# Once Upon
A Time and Stories
from Around the
# WORLD

# Once Upon
## A Time and Stories
## from Around the
# WORLD

By: Rosaria M. Wills

David Womack Wills (posthumously)

authorHOUSE®

*AuthorHouse™*
*1663 Liberty Drive*
*Bloomington, IN 47403*
*www.authorhouse.com*
*Phone: 1-800-839-8640*

*First published by AuthorHouse    08/03/2011*

*ISBN: 978-1-4634-4285-9 (sc)*
*ISBN: 978-1-4634-4284-2 (ebk)*

*Library of Congress Control Number: 2011913205*

*Printed in the United States of America*

# CONTENTS

# PREFACE
## Thoughts

Nostalgia is like a grammar lesson: you find the present, tense, but the past perfect (Pomeroy)

God gave us memories that we might have roses in December (Barnie)

We do not remember days, we remember moments (Pavese)

The past is never dead; it is not even past (Faulkner)

Every great dream begins with a dreamer. Always remember, you have within you the strength, the patience and the passion to reach for the stars to change the world.
(Harriet Tubman)

Sometimes we stare so long a door that is closing that we see too late the one that is open
(Alexander Graham Bell)

You tried and you failed. That is not important, try again. You will fail again, but at least you have tried
(Samuel Beckett)

If we compare the river and the rocks, the river always wins not because of his strength but because of his perseverance
(Buddha Gautama)

# CHAPTER 1
## THE EARLY YEARS

Once upon a time . . . but wait this is not a fable, this is the true story of the life of a little girl born on September 28, 1942 in a little apartment on the third floor in one of the streets (Vicoli) in Naples. My mother told me that she went into labor just about when bombs (she kept emphasizing American bombs) were dropping nearby. One hit the local postal office and at that time, I was born. My brother (12 years older than me) when he saw me, his first reaction was, "Come e' brutta" (boy is she ugly). As my mother told me, I was all eyes, no hair, certainly not a beauty. My mother told me I looked like a bird. She wanted to call me Isabella, but at the moment of my coming in the world, my mother was praying so intensely to our Lady of the Rosary that she decided to call me Rosaria Maria. Our lady of the Rosary is in Pompei (a town near Naples), a beautiful sanctuary and attached to it an orphanage. Pompei and Ercolano were destroyed in 79 A.D., during the Vesuvio's eruption. My mother used to tell me that she had hoped that her child be born with a beauty mark on her left cheek. I do not know if she told me, so that I would not be conscious of my mole on my left cheek or if she really wanted to. I don't have any baby pictures. My first picture was taken when I was 5 years old. We didn't have any monies, milk lacked, food lacked. My mother used to smuggle olive oil on the black market to make money. She would be carrying huge containers of oil while the Germans will be shooting and sell it on the black market with my father.

My mother used to tell stories of her life as a child. Her father was a strict Colonel of the Carabinieri. (The King of Sardinias, Vittorio

Emanuel I by Royal Warrant on 13th July 1814 instituted the Carabinieri in Turin. It was given the dual function of national defense, in first position with respect to other branches of the Armed Forces, and policing with special powers and prerogatives. The Carabinieri Force was issued with a distinctive uniform in dark blue with silver braid around the collar and cuffs, edges trimmed in scarlet and epaulets in silver, with white fringes for the mounted division and light blue for infantry. The characteristic hat with two points was popularly known as the "lucerna". The force was organized into divisions. They were called companies and sub-divided into lieutenancies, which commanded and coordinated the local stations, and were distributed throughout the national territory in direct contact with the public. On January 24th, 1861 the Force was appointed "First Force" of the newly founded national military organization, rising to the status of Armed Forces on 31st March 2000. The privileged position, as well as the presence of Carabinieri in every part of the country, even in the smallest village, were and still are the most significant characteristics of the Institution. (When you applied to become Carabinieri they looked back at 6 generations)

Apparently my mother was not an angel when she was a child. Her father (Raffaele) decided to place her in a school run by nuns. She told me, she got in all sorts of trouble. One day, she was at the altar cleaning, when she decided to see what the wine that the priest takes during the mass tasted like. So she took the wine and drank it. It was the Lacrimae Christi (Tears of Christ), very expensive wine, and she replaced the missing wine with water. The next day, during the mass, the priest reached for the wine, after the first sip he could tell it was water; he looked directly at my mother. The nuns punished my mother, by making her kneel on kernels for two hours. She said it did hurt. The father was called and asked to take the daughter back as incorrigible. He then placed her in a public school. My grandmother, Amelia, (born in Florence, she died in Naples) was a famous tailor. She was always traveling to Paris and Cannes in France to present her fashion. My great-grandmother, Clorinda Davini Giuliani (maybe related to Mayor Giuliani), was an Italian professor. My grandmother died at 48 years old of a heart attack, my great grand mother died at 79 years old, with pneumonia. She took a bath in the winter with cold water. My grandfather died in 1950, I do not know of what. He had disowned my mother, and left his wife.

My mother, my grandmother and great-grand mother lived in Lucca, where my mother was born, right next to Puccini's (a great composer) house, so she was able to get free tickets to operas. (Giacomo Puccini was born in Lucca on Dec 22, 1858. He died in Brussels, Belgium on November 28, 1929. (Dave was born on November 15, 1929). His most famous operas were "La Boheme", "Tosca and "Madama Butterfly"). My mother loved opera. My grandmother had white hair by the time she was 30 years old. My mother told me, that during a very bad storm, a lightning had entered the house thru the chimney, swept all around, burning some items, and my grandmother got so scared that her hair turned white. I am not sure how much truth was in that, but it was a fascinating story, and my mother was afraid of storms. My mother, Maria Antonietta, (she kept saying that she had the same name of the Queen of France who had been guillotined during the French Revolution) did not have an easy life as a child. Her mother hated her because her husband wanted a boy and when she had a girl, he was quite angry. So few years later he left his wife and child. Her grandmother adored her and protected her as much as she could. My mother had a very rough life when she was growing up and later in life.

A neighbor gave me the news of the death of my father. I did not know my father was dying of prostate cancer. I thought he was away for work. One neighbor approached me (I was about 5 years old), and said, "Poor thing, your father is dead". My mother was so furious. I cried for days. Then I dreamed of him, he was a skeleton and talking to me. I was so terrified, that in my dream I said, "Please do never come again in my dreams. I am too scared." Since then I have never dreamed my father again. In Italy when you have a dream, each vision has a number that you can play at lotto. My mother talked with a friend of hers, explained my dream, and three numbers where played, and it won, just 3000 lire but at that time it was a lots of money.

# WAR

I have no recollection of these days since I was a baby, my remembrance are based on what my mother used to tell me. I did have dreams of having my mother carrying me running, under the "ricoveri" (underground places) to escape bombs when the warning sirens came on. Germans were not very nice with the population. My brother, who was blond and blue eyed, was often mistaken for a German. My mother was from the North part of Italy (Lucca) and people in the North are blond and blue eyed due to the Longobard invasion, while people in South Italy are short with dark eyes and dark hair, due to the Spanish influence. My mother was always called "Forestiera" (foreigner) because she had been born in the North. My father, Amedeo, had been born in Bari (called the Florence of the South). My brother was a twin. My mother couldn't take care of both of them, so his brother was in care of a babysitter. My mother did not know that this lady was not feeding the child appropriately. The twin brother died for lack of good food and poor health. My mother thought that when I got married I would also have twins, or Marilou would, maybe Alessandra will.

She told me that one day during Christmas my brother was walking home and a group of Neapolitans started chasing him and screaming, "German, German." My brother ran to the house and hid under the table until my mother was able to explain to them that he was not German but Italian.

During the war, before I was born, my mother went with my small brother to Aversa (a little town on the outskirt of Naples). The Germans went to this little town and since one of the villagers had killed a German soldier, they made all the Carabinieri dig a hole and they shot each one of them one at the time, while the next Carabiniere would cover the body of his friend. There were hard times as I was told, she used to strain potatoes peelings to make soup, and eat vegetables instead of meat. Tough times, all neighborhood destroyed. When finally the Americans landed, the Neapolitan had had enough of the Germans, and in the famous 4 days of Naples, from September 23 thru September 30, 1943 the Neapolitans kicked out the Germans by throwing furniture even toilets out of the window on the tanks, many people died, but the Germans left the city before the Americans actually arrived. My brother was not an angel, while in Aversa, he and his friends decided to give wine to some chickens. The poor chickens got drunk and were walking around running in each other. He got in a lot of trouble.

My mother went thru two wars WWI and WWII. She was very scared of the Moroccans; they had taken women including nuns and raped them as they went thru villages. Everyone in Italy had many stories to tell; I would imagine that the war caused many psychological problems in many people. My mother every time she heard a plane, she still thought that they were going to drop bombs, and she did not like to ride in an elevator or be in crowded areas, kind of claustrophobia . . . . she had nightmares for many years to come. Again it would be terrible to see friends dying or being shot for no reason. There were many stories going around, like Germans throwing babies in the air to practice shootings. I cannot imagine anyone doing this, but I wonder if the babies were not Jewish therefore there could be some truth. My mother told me she had met Mussolini when he was in power. A very interesting historical note, (papa would have loved this) Mussolini and Arturo Toscanini (great director) were not really friends. Toscanini was antifascist. When Toscanini was directing the Turandot in Florence, Mussolini had been invited to attend, but he said he would go only if Toscanini would first play the Fascist Anthem. Of course Toscanini refused. Mussolini did not go to the theater but during the interval he send a bouquet of flower saying "From Mussolini to Puccini (Puccini had written the Turandot)."

My mother was a beautiful woman. When she was young she resembled Greta Garbo, a movie star, and a sculptor had made a sculpture of her hands. She knitted very well; she knitted me a nice winter coat, and later she knitted all my babies' clothes. I cannot knit, I did learn how to macramé and made all the curtains at my Peachwood Lane house, in Florida.

I was not a very healthy child, probably due to lack of vitamins and good milk. I don't remember much about my young years, except that I went to school. (My elementary school was in an old building. The name of the school was Principessa Mafalda. Princess Mafalda was the 2nd daughter of Vittorio Emanuele II and Elena di Savoia. She was born in Rome on November 19, 1902. She knew Puccini.)

I did have some friends, some that I did not care for much, but we had no money for food, we were on welfare, and this people will feed me many times. When I was about 6 years old, I disappeared with a friend. We had decided to go to the Giardinetti (park) to play. We had not told our mothers, dark came upon us and finally we came back home to our worried mothers. My mother really punished me (after she hugged me) for good reason. I also loved to slide between the staircase rails, till I got too old to do it. I didn't need a lot to be happy.

My mother worked by filling up forms for Ada's father (Rosetta's sister, I will talk about Rosetta in more details later on). Ada was very unhappy because she wanted to make the money, so my mother lost that tiny job. She did have some money that she lent to people, and I went to collect the money every week with 20% interest. It was dangerous because lending money with interest was against the law, but everybody did it.

My brother did not save money, with my teaching (I'll talk about later) I did save quite a bit, so I loaned money to my brother and I charged him 20% interest. He always paid me back.

My mother did odd jobs, including cleaning apartments, to feed us. My brother, Dominic, nicknamed Mimmo, joined the Carabinieri mainly because my mother was worried that he was going with a wrong group. He did not like school, and was having hard time passing classes. The first time he applied for the Carabinieri he was dismissed because they said he had not passed the physical (disfunzione alla tiroide, thyroid problems). My mother talked with Colonel Favella and was able to make him retake the physical and this time he passed (the fact that his grand-father had been a Colonel in the Carabinieri also helped). Mimmo was sent to Sila (in Calabria). He was a motorcycle policeman and enjoyed it. We used to go there every summer when school was out. We will take a train, but for some odd reasons my nose always bled. We will stay in a little pension, which also provided food (all for free). I was very thin and did not eat very well. We will take long walks (my mother and I) in the woods. One day I was picking fruit from the roves and a snake was standing right in the bushes. My mother pointed at the snake and just froze. I looked at the snake, took my mother by the hand and start running. Some people drove by and I kept saying, "Snake, snake." Everyone thought I was joking. We never walked again in that area. Sila is very famous for snakes, especially vipers that you cannot see, since they are so tiny, but their poison is fatal. There was a legend saying that a group of soldiers were in the woods for training, one soldier had done something wrong, and so his superior had tied him to a tree as punishment. A snake approached, he started screaming but no one listened. The next morning they found him with his mouth open and a snake sticking out from his mouth.

Sila is a beautiful tourist place; each chalet is made of different forms (bananas, a pear, an apple and so on).

Because of my nose bleeding my mother took me to the doctor. The doctor said I had a mild case of tuberculosis (pleura) and prescribed horsemeat. It tested funny and above all was very expensive. My mother also fed me everyday a raw egg that the farmer would bring to the house.

I did not eat spaghetti till I was married. Mimmo used to say they looked like worms, then he would place pepper on them, and say, "Look ants". I will disgustedly put the food away, and my brother would go ahead and eat it, till my mother found out. My brother got punished and he stopped teasing me. When Mimmo was young (my mother used to tell me), he used to get up in the nights, as he was sleepwalking and go to the kitchen and eat. My mother really thought he was sleepwalking, till one night she followed him, and she saw him opening one eye to see where the food was. He got punished. He also used to talk in his sleep. My mother would ask all kind of information about school and he would answer them, then the next day my mother would say, "so you got a bad grade on your test" and he would say, "how did you know". I wonder if he is still talking in his sleep.

# My well justified fear of camping out and picnics

One day my mother and brother decided to go for a picnic at the Floridiana, a park in Vomero. Because of my fear of ants, I placed a large white sheet on the grass, so I could see if ants were coming. My mother and brother both laid down on the grass, sleeping away, all of the sudden I started screaming, ants where coming towards me right on the white sheet. I ended up standing up all thru the picnic. Never went to a picnic again.

Mimmo had a friend his name was also Domenico. While Mimmo was 6 feet 1 inch tall, his friend was 5 feet 6 inches. They looked strange when they were walking together. My mother used to call them, "Il pane e la giunta" (the bread and a little bite).

Mimmo kept complaining about staying in Calabria. My mother made me write a letter to a General, asking him to have my brother moved to Naples since he was the sole provider of the family. After few months, the General's assistant wrote back and my brother was transferred next to us. We were very poor, the rent was 2,000 lire a month ($2.00) and we scrambled for food and clothes. These were the times when a candy will cost five lire, less that half a penny. My brother would send us a check every month for 5,000 ($8.00) lire and it did help.

I loved to dance, so when my friends had parties at their house I would go. We could not have them at our house, because we had no music box, neither enough room. When I went to my friend's house for a party, everyone wanted to dance with me the tango, the walzer, the twist and the cha cha cha. I was really good at those dances. I loved ballet, so I will stand on my tennis shoes and try pirouettes. I dreamed to become a ballerina. Dream is the key word. Taking ballet lessons was an impossible dream.

In Italy at Christmas instead of Santa Claus we have the 'Befana' (a good witch). She would come on the 6th of January, and would hide the toys all over the house. Our house (apartment) only had two rooms, a kitchen, a bathroom (which was in the kitchen) and no shower. (We used a big pan with cold water to bathe, once a week.) I believed in the Befana till I was 11 years old. I used to stay awake throughout the night to see if I could see her. I would hear noises and would hide under the covers. I had asked for ballerina shoes, instead I received a gold ring. I was so angry. Later I lost the ring. (On purpose, who knows?) We also had a traditional Presepe (Nativity Scene), with shepherds, mountains, lake, it was beautiful, and we worked very hard on it. I don't know what happened to it.

I received my first Communion and Confirmation the same day. I looked really pretty in the white dress. My brother could not come, we did not celebrate very much, but my godmother and godfather took me to their house and we had a very nice dinner. The only thing that hurt was that my mother had not been invited and she couldn't join us for dinner. (These people were relatives on my father's side).

One year my mother sent me to summer camp for health reasons. The doctor had recommended mountain air. I detested going, I had never been away from home. It was in the mountains but you could walk to the sea. I learned how to make straw baskets with pine needles. I hated to take showers with all the other girls, and the nuns made us lay on the ground without a top to take a suntan. I loved egg yolks, and all the other girls will give me their egg yolks. I cried every night, sleeping in that big room with so many people. I had won a Dr. Jackal and Mr. Hyde book and someone stole it from me. It broke my heart. I cried for days, it was the first time that I had won anything.

I used to write to my mother, but the nuns read our mail, so I'll say in the letter, "It is so nice here, I love it, come and get me." She never did, it was for my own good and my health did improve.

I would say a prayer every night, the same prayer that I learned when I was 5 years old, I still say it.

It goes like this:

A letto a letto me ne andai

Quattro angeli sognai

Due al piede, due al capo

Gesu' Cristo al mio lato.

Gesu' Cristo che mi disse

Che dormissi, che riposassi

Che paura non avessi,

Ne' di giorno, ne' di notte

Ne' sul punto della morte

(Translation: I am going to bed, and I am dreaming of 4 angels, two at the feet of the bed, and two at the head of the bed, and Jesus at my side. Jesus tells me to sleep, to rest, not to be afraid, during the day, the night, or when I am approaching death).

Across from our building lived an old lady (probably she was not old, but at my age everyone seemed old). We used to call her the Cat's lady. She had cats after cats in her house, forever feeding them. She also was up to date with all the gossip in the neighborhood, so my mother would stop by and talk for hours. It was extremely boring.

I was always a loner. When you look at some of my early pictures you can see sadness in my eyes. I used to pray every night that my mother would not die, and pray to God to let me die first. I did not want to loose my mother and be by myself. While I prayed I silently cried, since my mother and I shared a big bed.

## A good Friend-Rosetta

Rosetta' mother had been a longtime friend of my mother. Both mothers used to go to the park when my brother, Mimmo, and her daughter, Ada, were babies, but they had lost track of each other. When I went to the Middle School, Pimentel Fonseca, (the school was named after Eleonora Pimentel Fonseca, she was born in Rome on the 13th of January 1752, and her parents were Portuguese. At 10 years old the family moved to Naples and thanks to her uncle she was able to study Greek and Latin), I met this girl Rosetta. I told my mother about my new friend, and she recalled her mother. So they met again, and we became best friend. She was very strange but nice and good hearted. She did not like to study, and her mother, Eva, used to compare her to me, by always telling her. "You should be more like Rosaria, (at that time they called me Maria. My name is Rosaria Maria, my mother was also Maria, and so they used to call us big Maria and little Maria. I hated it, so when I was about 12 years old, I said, "my name is Rosaria, if you call me Maria I'll not answer." It took a while for my family to get used to it, but they accepted my decision), studious and quiet." Eva also said, "Acqua cheta rompe I ponti" (quiet waters break bridges). In few words I was quiet but I would be accomplishing something in the future. Her mother used to call Rosetta "cozzica" (clam) because she loved the sea and she had a dark complexion.

I did not know how to swim. Mimmo used to take me to the beach and my mother had told him to teach me how to swim. One day he took me by a rock in the middle of the sea, and swam away, and said, "Go ahead and swim back to the shore." Needless to say I was terrified; a young man swam by and I said, "Can you please help me and take me back to shore". He probably wondered how I had gotten to the rock in the first place. I love the sea but I am afraid of drowning. Rosetta taught me how to swim, by holding me up by the back of the bathing suit. I love the sea, I used to walk by the sea and watch it especially when it was rough and it rained. The sea is so quiet and so strong at the same time. In the summer since my mother did not like the beach, Rosetta, Ada (her sister), Eva (their mother) and I would go to the beach bringing either Frittatina (fried pasta), or Eggplant Parmesan, something that would not spoil. I would lay on the beach, relaxing and taking lots of sun. Rosetta was pushy, I did not like to argue so I went along in whatever she wanted to do, and just so I had a friend. I would call it now 'passive resistance'.

Eva was a faithful communist, she will go in the street to demonstrate against the government, but faithfully she would go to church every Sunday. Not a very convincing communist. She was also a heavy smoker and she loved long hair. I had long hair and when I went to her house, she will brush my hair and put her face in my hair. I really hated it.

Rosetta's uncle was a doctor. When Rosetta was 12 years old she had her tonsils taken out. Her uncle offered to take mine out also for free. I said, "No thanks, they don't bother me." Rosetta's aunt was in America and she would send Ada many presents, but not to Rosetta. Ada was the favorite one. Ada also played the piano. Rosetta and I used to sneak in the room, and play the piano while she wasn't there, then she found out and she started locking the piano. I learned how to play "Johnny Guitar", at that time a very popular song and I still remember it. Mimmo dated Ada for a while, but Ada was in love with Romeo (a doctor) whom she later married. (Eva could not stand him; she tried everything to break them apart).

With Rosetta we used to go to the movies. One time, this guy was sitting right next to me, and he tried to put his hand on my leg. I took a safety pin, and pushed it in his hand. He screamed, everyone started looking, and he left.

I used to envy Rosetta because she had a separate room in the house for the toilet, not just a toilet in the kitchen as in my house. If I went to the bathroom in my house in the night I was scared because we had roaches. In the winter I used to dress and undress in bed because it was too cold. We had a bag that we would fill up with hot water and place it into the bed to keep us warm. We did not have hot water, so we had to boil the water. My mother used to fill a bucket with coal to keep us warm.

I'll go to pick Rosetta up for school and she will always forget her books, and her mother would go screaming down the stairs yelling, "Rosetta, Rosetta, your books", Rosetta did not like school. When we walked to school, I would tell Rosetta: "Can you please hold my books for just a minute". She would take them and would talk away. When we arrived at the school, I would take my books back. It worked like a charm;

very seldom I carried my own books. At school we did not have lockers, we did not have class sets, nor back packs, we just carried the books and notebooks in our arms. When we finished Middle School, Rosetta and I separated. She went to a 2 years Technical school to become a bookkeeper, and I went to a 5-year technical school "Armando Diaz" (Diaz was born in Naples on December 5, 1861; he was an Italian general and a Marshal of Italy. Diaz began his military career as a student at the Military Accademy of Turin, where he became an artillery officer. He was a colonel commanding the 93rd infantry during the Italo-Turkish War, and Major General in 1914. On the outbreak of the World War I, he was assigned to the high command as head of the unit's operations under General Luigi Cadorna. He was promoted to 2-star General in June 1916, and assumed the command of the 48th division and the 23rd Army Corps. After the war, Diaz became a senator and in 1921 was given the title of Duca della Vittoria. In the same year Benito Mussolini named him Minister of War, and he was promoted to Field Marshal. Upon retirement, in 1924, he was given the honor of Marshal of Italy) to become a CPA. So we kind of drifted apart. We still saw each other, she had many boyfriends' problems, and she would ask my mother for advice. Her mother did not particularly care for Rosetta. I kept on studying. Strangely enough when Eva became sick with cancer and was about to die, she moved in with Rosetta not Ada, and Rosetta took care of her till she died.

## Varichina (Clorox) in the Eye

I was always a wispy girl. One day my mother sent me to the store to fill in a bottle of Varichina (Clorox) so she could clean some white clothes. I took the money, went to the store, and filled the bottle up. On the way back I decided to skip steps, and by doing so, I splashed the varichina in my right eye. It started burning, I started crying and running to my mother who immediately took me to the 'Pellegrino', Emergency Room, right next to the Church of Trinity. They washed my eye, and they said to be sure that I could see the next day. It was quite a scare, but I was all right. I always had problems with my eyes, I could not see well, but we had no money to buy glasses or even go to the eye doctor. In school I tried to sit as close as I could to the blackboard, so I could read the words, and squinted my eyes. It wasn't till I was 20 years old that I finally went to the eye doctor at the PX in Naples, for free (he was a friend). He checked my eyes, and said if I did not start wearing my glasses, I would be blind in few years. I wore very tick glasses. It wasn't till I got married and went to Germany with Dave, that at Trier I bought my first pair of contact lenses for $50.00 The German doctor thought that I would never be able to wear them.

They were hard contact lenses; I had hard time, but was able to wear them. I hated wearing glasses. When I read, I had to wear my regular glasses over the contact lenses. I lost these contacts many times. One time I was in the bathroom at work and one of the lenses fell off my eye (my eye was dry). I kneeled on the floor searching, searching. The contact was white and the tiles in the bathroom were also white. I finally found it, cleaned it and put it back in my eye. Many times the contact would get lost in the bottom part of my eye, and I had to literally search for it to place it back on the pupil. It was quite a chore. That's why when I came back to the States for good, years later I had my laser surgery done; now I only wear glasses when I drive in the night. I have always had trouble walking in the night. I can't see people's features, unless there are bright lights. The operation was expensive but certainly worth it.

Growing up I went to the Beauty Shop only once a year, at Christmas time. I will wash my hair once a week and then sit outside the balcony to let air dry it. One time I had lice; my mother took a thick comb and combed all my hair and got rid of the lice.

When washing clothes, there was no dryer or washing machine, mother did them by hand, and then she had a heavy string going from one side of the street across the other side and hung the clothes to dry. (You see the same in Brooklyn) She used to scare me, because half of her body would be hanging out in the street, but never bothered her.

Our bed mattresses were filled with pure wool. Every summer my mother had to take the seams apart and fluff the wool so that it would not be hard. When we came to the States, she brought her mattresses with her, and in the summer she would take the mattresses in the back yard and fluff the wool, till we finally talked her into having a new bed with a regular mattress and threw away the wool ones.

Since my mother was unemployed she would receive a welfare package at Christmas times, sugar, coffee, flour and pasta. It was a good thing, except many times you had to stand in line for three to four hours so you could get your free stuff. Before I was born she had been a Secretary at the Italian Navy Station, then the war started and she lost her job.

As I said before, I was very undernourished, ate mostly pasta, potatoes, beans, meat once a week. We went to the flea market, in Forcella, to buy used clothes; (the American people had donated these clothes to Italy to go to the poor. When the shipment got to the harbor, it was stolen and then sold at the flea market. I always believed that someone in the authority was being paid off.). My mother will fix them. A dress would cost around 50 lire (8 cents). I was embarrassed many times when I went to school, but we used to wear a Grembiale (an apron). In Italy we also wore a ribbon, in elementary school, different color for different grades, but in Middle School and High School just a black apron, so that I could hide the holes in my clothes. In High school we had many rich people and girls dressed up really nice.

When I was about 9 years old my mother had made friends with this family. They had a daughter, Giuseppina, and another friend. I used to go to her house; she lived in a huge apartment. She loved archery, so she taught us how to bow and arrow. I was pretty good at it. But if we did poorly she would pinch us and hurt us. I never told my mother. She had decided to run away from home and go to Africa and hunt big animals with the bow and arrow. The plan was to leave around 10 in the night, walk to the marina, steal a boat, and row across the Mediterranean to Africa. We thought it was a great idea, so we prepared for the big adventure. The night we were supposed to meet, I thought, "Boy is it dark outside, besides

I don't know how to swim." So I went back to sleep. The next day I found out, that the girl had actually gone to the Marina, tried to steal a boat, was stopped by a policeman, she was equipped with bow, lots of arrows, and a sack full of food. I was never allowed to go to her house again, and I have no idea what happened to the girl. (Probably in a psycho ward)

At the giardinetti, (park) I pretended to be a horse, and I would run down the hill making horse's sounds. Since I was almost an only child, I used to play by myself. When we had tangerines, I pretended that they were fighting a war, and when they lost I ate them. I always liked fruit.

My mother went to church every morning. It was a beautiful church in Via Roma with a catacomb underneath the church, where you could go and light candles. On Sunday we went to church. At that time you had to pay for chairs, around 50 lire. So many times we stood instead of sitting down. At Easter time all the churches will compete for the ones with the best flower arrangements. For Easter every one will dress up in their best clothes and walk down Via Roma, the principal street in Naples. We also had Easter eggs made of chocolate with inside a surprise. If you were engaged and wanted to give the ring to your future wife, you could go to the chocolate factory and order a special chocolate egg and place the ring inside.

## Some Italian Customs

In Naples, where I grew up, the custom at the end of the year was to get rid of the old stuff by throwing out the window. I don't know if they still have that custom. But everything that was not needed went out the window. Safer to stay inside, the next day the poor garbage men spent hours cleaning up. It was also bad luck if at midnight you were sitting down instead of standing. The next morning, on New Years Day if you heard a man's voice first it was good luck, if you heard a woman's voice was bad luck.

# Other Superstitions

In Italy, 13 is a lucky number, but 17 is unlucky. If you saw a hunchback, if he was a man was good luck, if was a female bad luck unless you saw three of them. You never placed a hat on the bed because someone will die. If your nose hitched a priest was about to die, if your hand itched, you would soon receive money. Just to mention a few. Of course breaking a mirror was 7 years of bad luck. Also wearing a horn and a horse shoe will bring you good luck. I have been wearing mine (a gold one) since I was 10 years old.

My mother used to read cards, and we will sit at the table and she would tell me what she thought might happen the next day. Each card meant something. I blindly believed in it.

In September we had a holiday called "Piedigrotta", (still do) it means at the feet of the cave. All children dressed up in costumes made out of paper, and then in the night they would have fireworks from boats in the sea. It was very nice. My neighbor, a tailor, used to make me these clothes for free; I have one picture, wearing one.

At Easter the priest will come to all the buildings and bless each apartment at no cost. I don't know if they are still doing that.

# Earthquakes in Italy

We needed money, so one of my jobs was to teach small children. I would sit all the children at the dining room table and teach them Math and Italian. I also taught bigger kids English; one boy kept flirting with me. One day we were studying and I was trying to make him say "fly" he kept saying, "flee". I hit him on the head and said; "say it right" He finally stopped playing around and said it right.

Two of the children I was teaching, were the sons of our portinaia (building keeper). Their father was a thief, but as he used to say, he only stole from the rich and not the poor and mainly stole from the Americans.

One day, his wife left the door open at their apartment, and someone entered the apartment and stole her husband's coat. She screamed all thru the building, how horrible this person had been to steal from her house. We all thought it was very sarcastic and funny. Anyway, I was there teaching, the children were sitting at the table, my mother was talking with a neighbor across the street. The apartment complexes were so close to each other that you could easily talk across the street. (My mother also used to look at the apartment across the street in the evening, hiding behind curtains. This couple will fight all the times, and my mother kept up with the gossip. I personally did not care). All of the sudden I noticed that the building was moving. I thought maybe my head was spinning, till I heard screams all the way down the street. "Earthquake, Earthquake". Everyone started rushing in the street. The children started crying. I lost my patience and told them, "Shut up; let me see what is going on." Then I opened the door and people were running down the stairs. I told the children to quickly go home. The staircase was full of people fleeing. I told my mother to wait. When everything seemed calm, we walked down the stairs to the Big Piazza (square) Plebiscito. It was full of people, we could see the Vesuvio smoking . . . then everything quieted down. Many people decided to sleep in the square, I didn't like to sleep on the ground (an ant complex), and I told my mother "Let's go back to the apartment, if we are going to die, let it be". So we walked home, slept soundly, since no one was in the building. Many buildings collapsed and people lost their homes. The building where we lived was over 500 years old and it stood up beautifully.

As I have said many times, we did not have any money. Once a month we used to go to one of my mother's friend who owned "La Scimmia" ice cream parlor, and he would give us two ice creams for free. (The place was still there when Dave and I went back in 1999, the original owners had died, and their children had taken over. When I told them my story, the new owners gave ice creams to Dave and me for free). I ate my ice cream really fast (still do), while my mother took forever to eat one. So we would be walking down the street, my ice cream gone and my mother still eating.

She would receive all kinds of stare, people thinking how mean of her not to give me an ice cream. My mother used to get very upset, but there was no way that I could slow down eating my ice cream. Dave also ate his ice cream very slowly. He used to say, "You cannot enjoy an ice cream unless you eat it very slowly." It was the same with chocolate bars. I'll finish mine in a moment, and Dave would still, as he said, savor his.

We had a very interesting postman, Don Vincenzo, he would read postcards when he delivered them. He would say, "Signora Caricchio, I have a letter for you from your son and a postcard, and he is okay." He was a very nice person, and he knew everyone's business.

At Christmas time in Italy, they have either chicken or turkey. You would go to the market and actually buy a live one, then go home, kill it and cook it. We always bought chicken since turkey was too expensive. So my mother would buy a live one to take home. One particular Christmas my brother was home, so my mother asked him to kill the chicken, my brother took the gun and started to aim it at the chicken to kill it. My mother stopped him and said, "You cannot do that, you need to twist her neck". My brother refused, he walked away, and so she took the chicken by the head, twisted her neck, and then cleaned it. What a sight. Also at New Year Day, in South Italy they eat the "Capitone", a heel. Again you buy it fresh. They looked like snakes and we never ate one. My mother also used to make her own liquor. She would buy alcohol extracts, (mandarin, lemon and so on) sugar and cook the whole thing on the stove for hours. It was cheap and quite good. At Christmas we also met with our friends and played Tombola (Bingo), using white beans or 5 lire. It was fun.

In Middle School I was the youngest one (I had skipped 5th grade thru testing at my mother's request). My Italian and Latin teacher, Ms. Bovenzi, was very tough, I did not have good grades in her class, I was sent to summer school (in Italy, there is no summer school per se, you study on your own, and then take a test and see if you go on or not). I passed.

While I was in 6th grade I decided one day during class to turn lights off in the classroom, while the teacher, a very handsome young priest was teaching theology. Obviously the teacher sent me out in the hallway. The

Principal came by and the first thing I could think of was to say, "I was sad, because today is the anniversary of my father's death, that's why I turned the lights off." And I started crying. The principal sent me back to the classroom saying it was okay and never to do it again.

One day was raining very hard, we girls were wet, and our stockings were wet, so we took them off and hung them by the window. When the same handsome young priest entered, his face turned bright red. Poor priest. Some girls on purpose would climb on the desks, with their short dresses, to pick something up. I would imagine he either asked for a transfer or left the priesthood. The school was an old building, but very well kept. It was in the middle of the city. It took a half an hour to walk to school at a fast pace. Buses were not available from my house. Students did get special rate to ride the bus. The school was next to a cathedral, and we will go there and pray before a test.

In school I was very good in the long jump and running and basketball. But in Italy sports had to be done after school and pay for it. We did not have the money so I couldn't enter any sport, even if the teacher thought I was Olympic material.

My school, especially High School, was very hard. Ms. Mattioli, my English teacher, took a liking to me and she was able to get me free books (In Italy you have to pay for books and tuition. I used to buy them all used). I used to go to her house, she lived alone with her sister, and she would fix me hot chocolate and cookies, something that I only had when was my name's day. In Italy we do not celebrate birthday as much as we celebrate name's day. Unfortunately Ms. Mattioli was deaf from one ear. She did not wear a hearing aid. The students knew that and they will talk away and pass test information from the side where she could not hear. It broke my heart, but I could not tell her because she was very sensitive of the fact of being partially deaf. I would tell my supposed friends that it was not right.

One teacher that I will never forget was my Merceology (chemistry) teacher, Ms. Esposito; she gave me pure hell thru the school year. If she asked a question, and I raised my hand to answer, after the first sentence, she would say. "I know you do not know what you are talking about, next." One day I was so angry that I picked up my ink box and was going to throw it to her, till my friend behind stopped me. I would definitely been expelled, and I certainly could not afford that.

I was not very good at drawing, one of my subjects. One day I received an "F" so my mother went to see the teacher. The teacher showed her my drawing and asked her, "What do you think this is?" My mother was speechless; she had no idea. The teacher went on, "It is supposed to be a butterfly, but as you can see it looks like a bra". My mother could not argue with that. When she went to see my teachers they all said the same thing, "She is so quiet, is she the one with the piggy tails?"

We did not have a cafeteria in school. We went to school from 08:00 to 12:30, but some days we had to stay in the afternoon for extra classes, so we were allowed to go out of the school and buy food, normally a small pizza filled with ricotta for about 50 lire (8 cents). The inside of the school and the stairs were all made out of marble. One day my friends were sitting on the balusters waiting for the time to go to class. It had rained all day, I was late, so I ran down the hallway to get to the classroom, the floor was slippery and I fell right on my butt, it hurt, but what it hurt the most was all the guys looking at me and laughing. If I could have, I would have died. Anyway with as much dignity as I could, I got up and went to my class.

In the school 'Armando Diaz', we had a Bar (in Italy a bar, has coffee, pastries, cokes and so on). It was only for the teachers; students were not allowed in unless they were sick and needed a coffee.

Everyone in Italy smoked, I did not, but my friend kept bugging me about smoking. So one day I took a cigarette from one of my friends, went to the restroom, and lighted it. I took one smoke, but instead of exhaling I inhaled, I got so sick to my stomach, threw the cigarette away, and I said, "Forget it". My brother did smoke but then he did quit.

Mimmo had a strange friend, he was afraid to go out during the day, he would go out only in the night (no, he was not a vampire) and rain or no rain he carried an umbrella with him.

I had some good friends, Rita, Concetta who was in love with Giuseppe. I think they did get married. I lost track of them, when I left school. Concetta's sister Maria did not like school and she quit in the 8th grade. She liked to cook. She was famous for her Polpettone (meat loaf), so when I went to her house to study with Concetta she would be cooking her famous Polpettone.

In our neighborhood my best friend was Vito (a young man) and Franco (whose mother was blind). I went to Vito's house and his sister Anna to play games. I exchanged comic books with Franco. Franco thought he looked like a rock singer and used to wear his hair the same way as his idol. He was a very nice young man. By now an old man, a good friend. I had more male friends than female friends.

My accounting teacher was the father of 8 children, very jovial, very interesting person and very helpful and very funny.

I had a fantastic Math and Physics teacher. He was an atheist, but he was an excellent teacher. His God was Einstein. He would give us a test every day by calling four students by his desk at the same time, to solve 8 problems. You had about 2 minutes to answer the questions without a calculator (at that time we did not have calculators in the classroom, I never owed one) before the next group would go up. We had to think fast. He used to talk about Hiroshima (1st atomic bomb) and about a little girl walking down the street with her eyes in the palm of her hand. We of course always said "uh . . ." (We never figured out how she could have walked down the street with her eyes in the palm of her hand, but it kept us from listening to two hours lecture). Our High School was on a block schedule, so once a week we had two hours of Mathematics, Physics, and Italian.

Our theology teacher came right after our Physic's teacher. They used to give each other dirty looks, and the theology teacher would tell us, "Whatever he is saying, it is wrong." Our physic teacher also said there is no such thing as hot or cold. The feeling is passed to us thru our nerve system, telling our brain when it is hot and when it is cold. We could control our brain by telling our self, "I'm neither cold nor hot" and presumably we would be comfortable.

In Italy students remain in the same class, the teachers move around from class to class.

During my High School, students went on strike to free Trieste from Yugoslavia. All students went walking arm in arm, down Via Roma chanting "Free Trieste". I was the only one that went to school that day, and the teachers went on with their lessons. I couldn't afford to miss school.

We had a dog, a very mean dog, which would bite anyone. If he got outside the door and saw someone walking up the stairs, he would bite him/her. We also had a pretty cat. For a while we also had chickens that laid eggs, till someone complained about them. We kept the chickens outside on the balcony.

My mother was always an early riser; she was up by 6 A.M. I'll be laying in bed sleeping away and she would start mopping the floor. I refused to get up till at least 11:00 A.M. on weekend. I laid awake in bed out of principle. I did not help mopping the floor. My job was to dust the furniture every week. My mother did the rest. My mother always took a nap in the afternoon about half an hour. Dave always could take naps. I wasn't ever able to just lay down in the afternoon, once I was up, I was up.

I wanted to be an airplane Engineer but I knew we could not afford college. Then I thought about being a Flight Attendant. I knew two foreign languages. I took French for 6 years and English for 5 years, but I was too short. At that time Flight Attendant had to meet certain requirements and that included height.

I also wanted to be a teacher but my mother wanted me to be an accountant. She thought I would be making more money. So I became a CPA, I studied all the times. I graduated in June and started looking for a job. I mailed more than 300 applications, but in Italy unless you have a recommendation or know someone, you cannot easily find a job. Also in

Italy jobs are passed from family members to family members. Example: Rosetta worked for the phone company; she retired earlier so her son could take her place at her job. I was also a chemist, but at that time only men were hired as chemist not women, in fact when I mailed one of my applications to a chemist industry, they answered by saying: "Sorry, it is a man's job, we do not hire women". If it had happened now, they could be sued for sex discrimination. (We used to test products to see if it had been modified, like quality control. The best part of the course was, when we had to check the wine; afterwards we could drink it if it was good). Everyone in Italy drinks wine. For children we dilute with water. We also drink cokes without ice and warm beer. Our national beer is 'Peroni' and is just awful.

At the High School they called me the "legs". I had beautiful legs and all the boys noticed that. At the end of the school year when we took a school group pictures, we used to have our schoolmates write wishes or comments on the back. Most of them wrote down "to the most beautiful legs in our school". I was embarrassed but they wrote it in pen and I still have the pictures. A boy, Enzo Castelluzzo, really liked me, but when I found out that he liked other girls as well, I dropped him. He was much older than anyone in class, and his eye will twitch when he was nervous.

I was very good in English and so I made many pen pals, some in Norway, Helga and some in England, Alan and one in South Carolina, Leon. We exchanged mail (even if mail was expensive in Italy). The boy from South Carolina, Leon, sent me a beautiful bracelet made of ivory (at that time it was not illegal to have ivory objects). I still have the bracelet. Helga sent me an old cross, which I still have; Alan loved Michael Cain's movies.

We took many school field trips mainly to Ischia and Capri. We did not have a graduation per se, we just said goodbye. Ischia is a beautiful island; you can buy huge lemons that are very sweet. Capri is famous for the Blue Grotto (la grotta Azzurra). Ischia and Capri were spared during WWII because the Germans loved to vacation there. To see the grotto you go in a small boat, then you have to squat down in the boat to enter the cave, the water is light blue, and you can see all the fishes. (Remembrance: when Dave and I went to Capri and Blue Grotto, I was handling the money, so I paid, and then I realized that I had paid too much so I told the guy in care of the boat: "Look I am not an American, I am Italian and I was born here in Naples, so don't try to cheat me." Everyone on the boat was a foreigner, had no idea what was going on, the guy gave me back the money. I told Dave later on what had happened.) You must be very careful in Naples. People are very good hearted but they will try to steal from tourists. When you have a car accident in Naples, or your car breaks down, many people will come to you with advice even if they have no idea on how to fix the problem. (Dave used to laugh about). In Europe we have the "Good Samaritan Law" where you have to stop and help someone on the highway, unless you want to receive a huge fine and go to jail. Italians always try to help. If you are lost and ask directions, they don't have the heart to tell you that they don't know, so they say, "Sempre diritto" (Always straight). Dave used to laugh at this sentence and used it himself quite often.

When I came back from school, I would first study, then my mother would fix supper, I would sit at the table, reading my magazine and eating, it infuriated my mother. But I loved to read and reading was an escape from reality on how poor we were.

I always had strong feet; my mother on the contrary had delicate feet. Every time she purchased a new pair of shoes, I broke them for her by wearing them for a while.

## My 11th Grade Prom Day with my brother Mimmo

I did not have a date; I went with my brother. It was wonderful. Our neighbor, who was a tailor, made me the dress for free, I just purchased the material, it was a copy of what Liz Taylor had worn in one of her famous movies. I danced all night with my friends, with Mimmo watching over me.

Everyone where I lived knew my brother was in the Carabinieri. One day I was window-shopping, I had my purse with me with 50 lire (8 cents). I was looking away and I did not realize that a Vespa with two young men was approaching very fast. They came by me, grabbed my purse and drove away. I was very angry. I went back to my apartment, knocked to our building keeper' door (remember the thief's wife) and I said "I know who took my purse, if I don't get it back, I will tell my brother and they will go to jail." She said, "Okay". I went back window-shopping, few minutes passed and the same Vespa came by and the young man said, "Here is your purse, we are sorry, we did not know who you were." My 50 lire were also intact in my purse.

Mimmo was always dating a different girl every time. One time he dated a German girl. She was so nice, and she bought me my first pair of Blue Jeans. I wore them for years. Then he dated a nice girl Nina (a very good tailor), but he could not marry her (his marriage had to be approved by the Carabinieri, and he could only marry when he was 30 years old), because all her family belonged to the Communist Party. They had to break up. I really liked her. (I have a picture with her)

When my brother got married in Calabria, we went to the wedding. I was pregnant; we stayed with Rosarina (my sister in law)'s family. One interesting thing, the toilet was underneath the sink, and you had to bend over to do your business. Dave could not believe it.

Carabinieri are quite powerful in Italy. Mimmo and I, never had to pay for movies, and many times we ate free in restaurant when he showed his badge.

One time Mimmo, my mother and I went to a theater show where a magician and hypnotist were performing. He was hypnotizing many people. When he walked thru the audience, and approached my seat; he looked me in the eyes, and walked away. I am a very nervous person and I knew if you let your mind wonder he cannot hypnotize you. I guess he saw that he couldn't perform on me, so he walked away. It was a very interesting experience.

## Trip with Mimmo on a Vespa

Mimmo came every summer for about 1 month vacation. This year 1956 he was very happy because he had just purchased a "Vespa". A "Vespa" is a motorcycle, uses little gas, and almost every one in Italy has one. There is place for only two people. So, Mimmo decided that we should take a two weeks trip down South of Naples. It was wonderful; we saw so many different places. But one problem occurred; he ran out of money, we did not have enough to stay in a hotel, even a cheap one. So that night we went to the local train station, and slept on the benches. Quite hard benches I would say. Besides, the lights were on all night and there were some big bugs flying around (like the palmetto bugs in Florida). I had and still have a phobia about bugs of any kinds. (Surprisingly enough I don't have a reaction to the European mosquitoes, but I do with the Florida mosquitoes.) Needless to say, my brother slept like a rock, I stayed awake all night. In the morning before all the passengers would come in, we left, and made it at home. When my mother heard about this, she was not pleased with Mimmo. At that time we did not have cell phones nor telephones in the house, we had to go to the Post office to make phone calls, so there was no way to get in touch with anyone. Personally I thought it was wonderful, riding thru the wind, and feeling the breeze. It was one of the best times in my life. Later on Mimmo bought his first car. He would park it underneath our building and will get up during the night to check on it and every morning he would wash it. We thought it was quite funny and we used to pick on him about it.

My mother used to go down the street, where there was a newspaper stand, and spent hours reading the paper while standing there, a cheap way to read the newspaper.

Saint Gennaro, Naples's patron blood was and still is kept in the cathedral, and twice a year the blood would liquefy. If it did, it would have been a good year, otherwise a bad year. No one was allowed in the church except dignitaries, so we really don't know how much truth was in this.

I bought my first camera when I was 16 years old, a Kodak for 5,000 lire (about 8 dollars). I used it till 1980. Worked like a babe. Dave instead loved to take slides. We had a projector and the kids enjoyed watching slides.

Since Naples was a Sea Port, we had many American Aircraft Carriers stopping by. Mimmo had made friend with Lt Cavanaugh, so I was able to go on the aircraft carrier "The Intrepid". The young officer took me all over the ship. I had forgotten to wear pants so I was wearing a nice skirt. Joe Cavanaugh asked me if I wanted to climb in the plane, I said, "sure", he then realized I was wearing a skirt; he made all the sailors turn around while I climbed in the plane. I still have a picture that was taken at that time. I had a crash on Lt. Cavanaugh and I think he had one on me, but he knew my brother and he knew I was too young.

On Sunday, my mother and I used to walk all the way to Margellina right by the coastline, and some time look at the Luna Park (an entertainment place). I could not go on for lack of money, but it was nice to watch.

I was 16 years old when we finally purchased a small black and white TV. What a joy. I spent hours watching all the shows. At that time we only had 3 channels. The government owned and still owns televisions and radios stations and you had to pay a yearly fee.

## Desperately Looking for a Job

My mother and I were walking and saw many American cars. We had an idea. We took down their license tags numbers and wrote letters mailing them to the license plates owners. I was lucky because one reached a Mrs. Hoffmann, which was secretary to the General in NATO. She found me a job on the base in a shoe shop with the Sannino sisters. I learned how to type on my own, that is why when I type I only use eight fingers but I am very fast. I knew shorthand, which was different from the American shorthand. I enjoyed working in the shoe shop but I hoped to move up. When I started working, I had to take a Funicolare (an above ground subway), and then walk quite a bit to get to the NATO post. It was a very good exercise, not that I needed any; I weighted 98 pounds.

While working in the Shoe shop, two sailors kept bothering me to go out on a date. I kept saying, "No". Finally I got tired, and I gave both of them a date, to meet me at a certain square, same time and same hour. They both showed up, they did not know each other, they were standing next to each other. I was watching from a distance, and really enjoying it. It was mean, but they finally stopped asking me.

A job opened in the Briefing Room, in the main Headquarters. It was a better job, and a better pay. I had to take care of the meeting room, setting up charts, coffee and be sure that all the officers had the right material. They had meetings every Monday. Sgt Tarshes was my direct supervisor; he was married with an Italian lady. A big huge bear man, he sold watches on the black market for extra money. He took a liking to me and later introduced me to Dave. (Tarshes had told me, that I should never date an officer, they were dumb, and I should date a Sergeant). I had made friend with Paul Constantino. He bought a kormangia (a German car). And he would be singing before the arrival of the car. "Oh, mamma, mamma mia, where is my kormangia." (When I got married his mother send me from Ohio the wedding veil). He also came and visited Dave and I at Shaw Air Force base, in South Carolina.

One day a job opened in Intelligence for a bi-lingual secretary. I was not much of a secretary but I was bilingual. (English and French)

To work in Intelligence for NATO you had to have special clearance, and be investigated by the FBI. It took 6 months before I was approved and then they gave me a 'Cosmic Top Secret's clearance. (Higher clearance than Dave had. I used to pick on him about it).

Dave was going thru an ugly divorce; his wife had cheated on him with some of his best (?) friends. I tried to talk him in going back to his wife. We used to meet at the Snack Bar. I had told him that my family was from Florence, so one day he said, "my friend, his girlfriend and I are going to Florence; would you like to join us?" I had never been to Florence. So I said, "Okay". The day of the departure I showed up with my mother and two suitcases. He told me after being married, that he never thought I would bring my mother with me, and I never thought that he meant for me to come by myself. I used to joke and say, "Dirty old man, what did you had in mind". I saw snow for the first time. I had lots of fun. One strange thing occurred while at the hotel, we had one room, Dave and his friends the other two. I walked in his room and Dave was cleaning the toilet. I asked: "What are you doing, isn't the maid supposed to clean the toilet?" He said, "My friend here says that in Italy when you stay in the hotel, you clean the toilet yourself." I laughed and said, "He has no idea what he is talking about, stop cleaning, there is no such custom." He stopped.

We also went to Montecassino, about one hour from Naples. We had a wonderful day. (It was the place where most of the WWII fighting had taken place.)

We also went to Rome (only two hours away from Naples). I had never been in the Vatican City. There was a Mass going on, and the Pope was there. We were in the back of the church. I could not see what was going on, so Dave picked me up so I could see. A young priest came by and said in Italian, "Sir, this is not allowed, please place her down". We were quite embarrassed, since every one was looking at us. We saw the 'Pieta' by Michelangelo, (I just recently read that the 'Pieta' is the only masterpiece that Michelangelo signed his name on Maria's belt. Some other artist was trying to get credit for the statue) and the treasure of the church, given by Kings in the past centuries and an 18 karats gold Baby Jesus. It was quite impressive and wonderful. We also saw the Sistine Chapel (Cappella Sistina), the official residence of the Pope in the Vatican City. Michelangelo had been commissioned by Pope Julius II in 1508 to repaint the ceiling. Michelangelo preferred to sculpture and he refused. The Pope put him in jail till he would change his mind and paint. The work was completed between 1508 and 1512; most of the painting was done by Michelangelo laying on his back. On the way to Naples, we stopped at Via Appia. This is where Spartacus and all the slaves had been crucified. Spartacus was from Thrace, served as an auxiliary in the Roman

Army in Macedonia. He deserted the army, was outlawed, captured, sold into slavery and trained to be a gladiator. He escaped with other 70-80 gladiators. Fought the Romans, was caught and placed on the cross with all his men. This was normal punishment during the Roman Empire. Dave dug out two paving stones (we still have them).

These paving stones had been hand carved by slaves during the Roman Empire. Dave later painted them in gold.

While we were dating, Dave used to park his car by the golf course on the base. He was a very good golfer and won many trophies, which later on our children destroyed except for one. While he was playing golf someone hit the windshield of the Rambler and cracked it. Nobody had seen anything. The cost was $75.00; Dave did not have the money. So I lent him the money, and till years later, I kept saying, "You never paid me back my $75.00". His answer was always, "I owe you, and as long as I owe you we will be together."

Dave took me to the Flamingo Club for a date; I had never had a martini, so he decided I should try one. I started drinking, half thru the drink I started crying. He asked what was wrong. I said, "I don't want to die". He decided no more martinis for me. It was at the Flamingo Club during a Bingo game that we heard of the death of President Kennedy. Many people were crying; the whole base went on alert, for fear of someone taking over the government.

We also climbed Mount Vesuvio and looked in the crater, quite a walk (at that time Dave had no problem with breathing). We also went to Pozzuoli, (later on this is where we lived after married and where Bill was born) a city next to Naples. There is a solfatara, whose elliptic crater has a major axis of 770 meters and a minor one of 580 meters. It was formed 4000 years ago and is the only one in the Philegraean Fields, which still exhibits an impressive fumarolic activity. In the crater you can observe such interesting phenomena as jets of sulphurous steam, small volcanoes spitting hot mud and bubbling jets of sand. The last eruption of the Solfatara is calculated to have taken place in 1198 A.D. There is also a grotto called the 'grotto of the dog', because if a dog entered this grotto he would die due to a poisonous gas, but people could walk in it, and we did. We also went in the catacombs, where Christians will go and pray and arenas were the Christians would be fed to the lions. The arena was the Coliseum, where also fights between gladiators took place. The Coliseum has long been regarded as having been the scene of numerous martyrdoms of early Christians. We went to Roccaraso, a skiing section next to Naples. We also went to Caserta. Caserta is next to Naples; there is a Royal palace, which was built from 1752-1774. It took 3000 workers, mainly slaves and prisoners. It has 1200 rooms and 1970 windows. I would hate to have to wash these windows. The Americans used this royal palace during World War II for the troops. We had a chance to go to Sicily, to Palermo taking across a ferryboat. We ate at a restaurant but unfortunately their spaghetti was too much al dente (not truly cooked, actually raw). Also on the way down to Sicily we took Rosaria (future spouse of Mimmo). She had failed to tell us that she could not stand car motion, and so she threw up all over the back seat. What a smell, if she had just told us that she was getting sick.

Dave would talk about his staying in Alaska; he had been there and encountered many bears while there. He was in a bowling league, and one day while throwing the ball, he had hurt his back (the discus). He could not move for quite a while. For then on he had back problems, sometimes he could not walk straight. He would lay on the bed, and I'll pull his legs till both heels were equal. They were thinking of operating, but Dave did not want to. He did get better, but once in a while it would start again. He had been to Morocco (Dave used to come to my school during open house to keep me company. Three years ago this lady with two children came, and said that her father was from Morocco. Dave could not hear very well, but he heard the word Morocco and started talking about when he had been there, how poor the country was, how people were not very clean. I tried to change subject, but did not work. The lady was kind enough not to be insulted, but just agreeing with him).

I was the only girl in the Intelligence office, and I was treated like a queen. I used to play tricks on a Navy Commander (his wife and I set it all up). He used to keep chocolate bars in the desk drawer. So in the morning I would go in the drawer and take one piece of chocolate and leave a message, "The Black Hand strikes again" The Black Hand is the Italian mafia. He would go bananas, "Who is taking my chocolate; we have no Mafia in this office". He would place the chocolate in a different drawer, and then again I will take it and leave the same message. It was weeks before we finally told him. We had a good laugh. I also was the secretary for two officers, one Turkish and one Greek. One was a Major and one was a Captain. At that time Greece and Turkey were not very friendly with each other, (they still aren't). So the Greek Captain would come to me and say, "I need this letter typed by tomorrow". The Turkish Major would hear this, and will come to me and say, "I need mine first, and I am higher in command". I would just take the two letters to my boss, Sergeant Hart, (side note: we used to be very good friends with Sgt Hart and his wife, till both his wife and I got pregnant. We both were exposed to German measles. The doctors gave us shots. Her baby was born deaf; mine was healthy. From then on she would not talk to me), and say, "Here you take it and you type it".

Never work in the same office with your husband or boyfriend. Anytime Dave and I had a fight, I would refuse to do his typing, and poor Sgt. Hart used to do it for me. My direct officer was a Colonel Guazzini. He was very vain and refused to wear his glasses. His reports had to be typed in extra large characters. No computer at that time. It was quite a chore and took twice as much time to type. His wife, who did not speak English, was a member of the Wives Officer's Club. So once a month, I had to go with her at the club and translate what they were saying.

The nice thing about working for NATO was that since our salary came from all different countries we did not have to pay income taxes, and also in the summer, we only had to work from 07:00: to 13:00 and then we could take the military bus and go to the beach.

I was in charge of opening 7 safes with secret materials, since I couldn't remember all the combinations, they had set them all up in the first safe,

I'll open that safe first then with the combinations in hand I would open the rest. It took about 15 minutes every morning.

At Christmas we always had an office party. Nice party. At one particular one, I approached someone from behind, slapped him on the back and said "Merry Christmas". He turned around with a big smile (he was the general in charge of the headquarters) and he said "the same to you". I could have died I was so embarrassed.

I also used to answer the phone by saying "This is the Intelligence office, hello to you sir, madam or what the case might be." We all thought it was funny. One day I answered the phone in the same manner, there was a silence. And then the voice on the other end said, "This is Colonel Brown". I quickly said, "Sorry, Sir, just a joke." He did not say anything but I stopped using that greeting.

We had a young airman that every day when he went to lunch he would say, "I'm going to lunch to eat some grunt." I had no idea what grunt meant, I thought it was food. One day, Dave, Major Bates and I went to lunch and I said, "Oh, I'll have some grunt." They couldn't stop laughing and they told me what it meant. I got really red and stopped using that word.

Once a year they had parades, it was quite a sight with all the different national military dressed in high uniforms; it was quite impressive. My co-worker was British, Elizabeth, and every other words she will always say, "bloody this, bloody that", and I picked it up and used it and still do. Bad habits are hard to break.

## The wedding days "October 24 and 25,1964"

No one in the office knew that Dave and I were dating. Only Sergeant Tarshes and Sergeant Hart knew. When I announced to the office that I was getting married, they all congratulated me and then asked, "Who is the lucky fellow". When I told them it was Sergeant Wills, they could not believe it. Dave had proposed to me and he had purchased a beautiful diamond ring. I was on cloud nine. He apologized that it was a small ring and promised me to buy me a bigger one later on. I always refused. The little one represented his love for me and that was for me the biggest diamond in the whole world. He did buy one in Turkey but I always placed it on my right hand, the one he gave me will never leave my left hand or my heart.

I thought the marriage was going to be a simple matter but it was not. Because we were both working for Intelligence, we had to be approved by SHAPE (in Paris) so we could keep working in the same office. It took over six months for the papers to be approved, and we changed the wedding date at least three times, and every time we had to re-do the invitations.

Dave had been previously divorced, so in order to marry me in church he had to first become a catholic. He went to church and studied with a missionary, Padre Pio. I think they spent most of the time drinking wine. Episcopalians and Catholics religions are very close to each other. Dave had been an altar boy and he had been in the choir. Finally after his baptism, confirmation and communion, all in one day, we had to find a church and we decided to go to the Cathedral in Sorrento. We got married twice. October 24, 1964 was our civil ceremony. We went to the courthouse. I made mistakes on the big register, writing my old name not my newly married name. Then my mother said to David, "we will see you tomorrow in church", and took me away. He couldn't believe that his bride was leaving him. But you have to be married in church the next day, if the wedding has to come thru. So I left.

Mimmo was taking me to the altar. When the music began, "The Ave Maria", we had both entered from the wrong door, and we had to turn around and start all over again. Rosetta attended the wedding. She was in charge of taking pictures. She was backing up on the altar and her hair caught on fire, surprising everyone including the priest. In almost all my outside pictures, there is a fat girl standing by us; we had no idea whom she was. I guess she just wanted to be in the pictures.

The day of our wedding, on the way to church Dave had a flat tire; he was late coming. After the ceremony, it had rained but there was a rainbow. I knew I had made the right decision in marrying Dave.

As a wedding gift Mimmo gave me a washing machine. I was so happy. No more washing by hand.

For the honeymoon we took 20 days off and went all over Italy.

During our honeymoon no hotels were available in Rome, our first stop. We finally found a villa outside Rome with a beautiful fireplace. It was certainly worth the wait, but it was quite late in the night when we arrived. When we went downtown Rome we made a point to go to the 'Fontana di Trevi' (custom said that if you threw a coin in the fountain you will be back to Rome). No hotel was available in Torino, there was a conference going on, we slept in the car and found out in the morning that we were right next to the local cemetery. We stayed with my brother; he was stationed in Moncalieri, a subdivision of Torino. He took us to visit the jailhouse, which was underneath the castle. In Venice we stayed in a very cheap hotel. In Piazza San Marco they were selling tapestries. I loved one of the tapestries. It was a Venetian lady with slaves around her, buying items from far away. So I asked the seller how much did it cost. He said 10,000 lire, (at that time $10) and I argued back I would give him 5,000 lire. For three solid days, I bargained with him, going as far as telling I had 9 children at home and could not afford 10,000 lire. He knew I was lying. Finally on the fourth day, he said, "Go ahead and take it for 5,000 lire". Dave was so embarrassed, but as I explained to him, in Italy you never pay for what they ask for, unless you go to a store with fixed prices. The fun of buying in the street is to argue with the seller. I still have the tapestry after 43 years. We also saw the "Ponte dei Sospiri". (It is called the Bridge of Sighs because during the Inquisition supposed heretics where placed in there and tortured, and you could hear their sighs).

Our first fight was during our honeymoon while in Trieste. Dave loved peanuts, he had just purchased some, and as he was eating them, he will throw the shells on the ground while we walked. I told him not to do it; he kept saying they would disintegrate in the ground.

We went to Vicenza, I was still not familiar with American dollars, so we went in the PX and I bought all kinds of earrings and bracelets. Dave did not have the courage to tell me, that it was expensive. When they said it was $50.00. I said, "Gee how cheap". I almost died when he told me the truth afterwards.

While driving up North, the windshield wipers on the new Rambler went out. In Italy in autumn it rains quite a lot. So here is Dave trying to drive. He placed a string on the windshield wipers, and while hanging from the car's window, I would pull the strings so that the wipers would move and Dave could see and drive. It was not fun at that time, but we laughed about afterwards. Then we went thru the Po Valley with a very thick fog. We couldn't see a thing. So here I am again, hanging out the car window, telling Dave how to keep distance from the edge of the road. We finally saw a truck driving quite fast and we started to follow his lights till we arrived at the hotel.

When I married Dave, he was a Technical Sergeant. He had been a Tech Sergeant for many years since there was a freeze on promotion. After we got married he was promoted to Master Sergeant. He was so happy.

In the fall of 1964 (we had just married), David was sent TDY to Frankfurt, Germany, so I took time off to go with him. We left; Dave gave me a map, and said, "You give me directions". I am terrible at directions; I tried to tell Dave, but to not avail. (By the way we used to call Dave the "Map Man". He always had a map in his hands and later when Marilou worked at AAA he forever asked for maps. Dave was always good at directions. Marilou and Alessandra are the same; Bob, Bill and I on the contrary are horrible on finding directions. Also when we went shopping, and the cashier would give us change, whatever change happened to be, Dave would mention what happened in that year in history. He was a brilliant historian). So he started driving, when we arrived in North Italy, I told him to take a left, he went, the snow was gorgeous, the street or lack of were hard to find, we were supposed to go thru Austria, Dave was sweating because it was so hard to drive, while I kept saying "Wow, how beautiful". Finally he said, "Let me look at the map". I said, "We are going thru this road with all xx across". "That means do not drive thru these roads in the winter. We are in Switzerland not Austria. How could you have missed the whole country?" I answered, "I told you I don't do well on directions." Anyway we finally arrived in Germany. I was pregnant and I had a craving for risotto (rice) with tomato sauce. It was nowhere to be found. Finally we found an Italian restaurant, risotto was not on the menu, but when I started talking to the owner, she immediately cooked the risotto just for me. By that time the craving was gone, but I had to eat it anyway. We stayed on base to save money, so we did not tell them that they were two of us. We both slept on a tiny bed made for one person. He finally finished with his work and we decided to buy a Christmas tree in Germany. Unfortunately they were very expensive, so we bought a shovel thinking perhaps we could dig one up in the mountains. We started driving thru Austria, and along the side of the highway they were some beautiful Christmas trees. We parked by the side of the road, and walked up the hill. Dave cut a couple, I did not like them, and so we stuck them back in the snow. Finally we found one that we both liked, so Dave cut it down. People driving by were blowing their horns, and we waved back at them. We took the tree down; it did not fit in the trunk, so we tied it on top of the car. It took Dave and I almost two hours, drivers still blowing their horns, and we thought, "How friendly are they, to blow their horn". Finally we drove away. At the Austrian border the guard asked us," "where did you get that tree". I started getting suspicious, so I said, "In Germany, my husband is in the Air Force". He said, "Go ahead then". When we arrived at the Italian border, the Italian guards asked us where we had purchased the tree. I answered, "In Austria". We drove away; we arrived at our home in Pozzuoli, with our beautiful tree tied on top of the car. Dave found out later that it is against the law in Austria to cut trees down, they are all numbered, and we were wondering what that number was. Thank goodness we had cut the tree above the number. In fact there was a fine and jail time. The tree stayed green till Easter, and finally in April we threw it away.

Dave made all our bedroom furniture. He liked black, so all our furniture was painted in black. We kept the bedroom suite till 1967, and actually we kept the night tables even longer. I always wanted fairy tale white furniture, so in South Carolina, we purchased my dream bedroom suite. It lasted all the way to 1990. (When we bought the new one, I gave some of my white furniture to Marilou; she loved it.) He also built a beautiful bar, which we kept all the way to 1990. He built one also for his friend, and his friend gave us a beautiful Madonna, made of silver from Spain, that I still have in the bedroom.

While in NATO, Dave went to many TDY. He was always appalled by the French Military. They would take their Chef to these military exercises, and the soldiers were served meals with wine, while the poor American soldiers would be eating MRIs.

While stationed in Italy, Dave had to go to Turkey (Ankara) for a TDY. My mother stayed at home with Bill. We took a Greek airline, it was the first time I had traveled in a plane. It was an old plane; I could see the ground, and the top of the mountains. Dave was trying not to scare me, but later on he told me that the pilot was flying way too low. We landed in Athens, Greece, stayed a couple of days, saw the Parthenon. There was a guy that wanted to sell me stamps (I collected stamps at that time), but he wanted too much. We argued for hours then he finally gave me the stamps for the price that I had asked for. Then we flew to Ankara, Turkey. Colonel Avdan (a Turkish colonel and a good friend) met us at the airport. As is European customs, he kissed both Dave and I on the cheeks. (Dave was so embarrassed he was in uniform). Anyway, he took us to the hotel, kind of run down hotel. Colonel Avdan also took us to a mosque. The only thing that I did not like was that you had to leave your shoes outside. But surprisingly enough we did get our shoes back. Inside the mosque was gorgeous; there were no seats, but a thick carpet, and a huge chandelier in the center. I think because of Colonel Avdan, we had no problems. Then he took us to a restaurant, where there were Belly Dancers. Children were also allowed in there. I had to go to the restroom, so I left the table. Unfortunately the sign at the door was in Turkish, (I can read Turkish, because you read it as it is written, but I had no idea what it said) so I entered the room, it was the men's room. The men all turned around and looked at me, my face must have turned bright red, and they all laughed. I went back to the table and said to Dave, "Please let's leave now," and I told him why. He laughed and said, "Forget it, they do not know you."

Then we went to Ephesus, (this is where our Lady, the mother of Christ, presumably had died). We took an old beat up bus, we saw a man with a mule so loaded with merchandise, that we could only see the donkey's head and tail. We passed thru villages. In one of these villages, each house had a stork nest on top of the chimney. We were told that storks came every year, built a nest, and than left, and came back to the same nest the following year. We arrived at Ephesus; they were armed guards everywhere. They told us, "if you touch anything they would shoot you". French nuns were in charge of the place. A girl in France had dreamed of this place many centuries before. Where Mary's home had been, it was now a chapel, and a fountain on the outside with holy water. We also saw what it was supposed to be the burial ground of St. John. It was very moving. It was a wonderful trip.

Dave still had some days of TDY. He went to work; I went around walking in the Bazaar. It started raining; in one of the window shop there was a beautiful umbrella covered on the inside with roses for sale. I went inside asked for the price. When he told me the price, I argued back that it was too high. After one hour of arguing, I purchased the umbrella for the amount that I had asked for (by that time, it had stopped raining). He thanked me; he said it had been a pleasure to do business with me. (Later on I left the umbrella at the Officer's club and it was stolen). We also met some Italian friends that owned a jewelry store; we bought some diamonds, presumably smuggled from Russia. We also bought some camel saddles to be used as bar stools, we carried them thru customs, and every time they had to look inside, to be sure that there were no drugs. Also I was told we were not supposed to buy jewelry, so I wore all the jewelry I had purchased. What a trip.

We used to have a cat in the house that used to do his business in Dave's military hat, till Dave threw him out for good. We also had a dog, a mean dog that would try to bite everyone including Dave. His name was Blackie; not very original since he was a black dog.

I was not very good on telling ranks, so one day someone stopped by the house to see if Dave was home. He wasn't. When Dave came home I said, "Oh, an officer came by to see you." "What rank", Dave asked. "I don't know but he had an eagle on his shoulder." Dave laughed, and he picked on me about this forever.

Bill, my first born, was my pride and joy. I was three months pregnant before I went to the gynecologist. I was embarrassed. The doctor asked why I had waited so long; I told him that I just wasn't sure that I was pregnant.

I had to work to help with the family, since Bill was born 9 months after we got married. Dave as a military man was not making very much, he also had to pay child support from his previous marriage. He would work as a bartender at the club after hours to bring more money, and go to the University of Maryland to get his BA; he planned to be a teacher when he retired. (Previously he had taught at the Intelligence School, in Denver, Colorado). He was really good at his job.

While pregnant with Bill, one of my cravings was to eat spaghetti with olive oil and garlic. I was still working in the office, so every day we will go to the Italian mess hall, and as soon as they would see me coming, the cook will have the spaghetti with garlic ready for me. I still wonder how Dave kissed me everyday. He must have really loved me with all that garlic.

Dave loved to bowl. He taught me and we entered a bowling league while in Naples, Italy. He was so happy because one time he had bowled a perfect game, 300, which is very hard to achieve. I was pregnant, and many times I kept score. The rule was if a bowler got 111 in the 7$^{th}$ frame, he/she would buy a drink for the scorekeeper. I always asked for a large glass of milk. I was famous for my milk drinking. My handicap was always high due to my poor abilities of bowling (in spite of Dave trying to correct me). But once in a while I would go wild and have a beautiful game, so I would win a trophy for the highest game with handicap. It used to upset everyone. I entered my last competition when I was 8 months pregnant. My mother had made me a pretty maternity dress, except that it was quite stiff, so it would pull up when I bended over. Of course in bowling, you have to bend over, so I must have given quite a show. I was bowling so well, that Dave did not have the heart to tell me, except for saying, "Don't bend so low". I won a beautiful trophy, but when Dave told me about my giving a floorshow to the audience, I was really embarrassed. But I won a beautiful set of silver candelabras. (I still have them)

The day before my water broke we had gone to the Flamingo Club, where they had all the food you could eat buffet. I ate like a little piglet, thinking I still had time for delivery. When my water broke, Dave took me to the hospital, I was sick like a dog; the nurse kept asking, "What on earth did you eat last night". I did not answer. My doctor believed that a pregnant woman should only gain 20 pounds (and if you gained more than 20 pounds, he would put you in the hospital, till you lost your excess weight), and I was exactly 20 pounds. My doctor was not there, but a younger doctor was there. I was in a lot a pain; they were complications, and the doctor kept saying, "let's wait" while he was on the phone talking with his girlfriend on an upcoming trip. The nurse gave me a Rosary to hold in my hands and prayed with me. Finally, after 22 hours of labor, my doctor came in, they had to use forcipes for Bill, and we thought we had lost him. When Dave reported this to the Commander, the young doctor was transferred to Alaska, before I could go and give him a piece of my mind. I remained in the hospital for two weeks with urinary problems. Bill was a big boy, and we called him Jumbo. Dave loved to play the harmonica; he was really good, even later when his breathing was difficult he could still play. Bill loved Hawaiian music, we had a record with all the Hawaiian music and when he was about to go to bed, we would play the record, and he would peacefully go to sleep. I had hard times changing Bill's diapers. At that time you had to use cloth diapers, disposable diapers were not available. Dave instead was very good in changing diapers. It took me a long time to learn it well. I did not like ironing. My mother had always ironed, and my brother ironed his own uniforms. He was extremely particular. I had already ruined one of Dave's uniform shirts by leaving a burned mark. We got in a fight; Dave's got mad, and started ironing his clothes and mine. I certainly was not upset, but I noticed that every time we had an argument, Dave would go ahead and iron his and my clothes. So I saw a pattern, and an opportunity. Every time I did not feel like ironing, I would start an argument; Dave would get mad and start ironing his and my clothes, till he figured it out. He laughed but kept on ironing, this time without any arguments. He also was good at sewing. My mother did all the sewing, but after she moved with Bob, Dave would go ahead and do some sewing for both of us.

Bill's godfather was Colonel Civetta, a good friend, but we lost contact when we moved. Dave extended his tour one more year. Normally the tour lasted three years.

In 1965 Dave's tour in Europe had ended. He had been transferred to Shaw Air Force Base, in South Carolina. We took TWA. It was wonderful. We did stop first in Madrid, Spain, beautiful country. We went to see a corrida. Because of the heat, Bill had diarrhea. Dave took him to the bathroom to clean him, there was no toilet paper, so he took two one-dollar bills to clean him with. When he brought him back to the seat, he still smelled, but we could not leave till the show was over. It was the Garcia Lorca's festival.

We stopped in New York, to visit one of Dave's friends. At bedtime, the friend would give his little son (2 years old) a drop of whisky. I asked him why. He said, "Well, he has trouble going to sleep, this helps him out". Poor child he probably became an alcoholic by age 5.

Driving down to Florida, we stopped at a restroom; Bill had to go. In the restroom Bill found a $5.00 bill. He was on cloud nine. For then on, he was expecting to find money anytime he went to the restroom. We also entered a shop, selling all kinds of fragile material, and Bill hit one of the vases, and it broke. The owner was kind enough not to charge us for the item.

Before going to Florida we decided to visit Dave's brother. We visited Ted and his family. My mom and I cooked for the whole family (including Virginia parents) about 15 people. I was quite upset, because while my mom and I were cooking in the kitchen, Italian sauce and so on, they were all sitting at the table talking, and never asked us if we needed any help. That is where we met Dave's brother Bill. I liked Bill very much. He was a perfect gentleman, and he spoke French. Bill had spent many years in France. He was an architect. He was supposed to draw the floor plan of our home when we settled down. Dave had told me that when Bill had decided to return to the US from France, he had checked in the airport, and jokingly said, "I have a bomb in my suitcase". The French police arrested him. When he said it had been a joke, the French did not think it was funny. They took his passport away, send him back to the US, and considered him "Persona non Grata". In few words he could never return to France. Virginia did not like him, because he had not paid for food while staying there. That day Dave and I went to the store and purchased all the food that we thought they might need. While sitting around, I heard from outside, all kinds of loud noises, and screaming. I asked what it was. I was told that on the hill there was a Baptist church and every Sunday, there would be a lot of yelling and screaming. I had no idea why. In Italy 99% are catholic and we never screamed or yelled, so people could hear us from over the mountains. It was quite interesting and new for me. We never heard or saw Bill again. He had left Virginia and Ted's house and gone to New York. He disappeared. We presumed he had died in one of the shelters, or someone had killed him.

Before going to Shaw AFB, we decided to visit Daytona Beach, Florida where Dave had spent most of his youth. Dave decided to go fishing on the pier. I did not fish; I was wearing my bikini (too early to see I was pregnant with Bob). Dave wanted a beer; so he asked me to go to the bar at the end of the pier and get him one. I was wearing my big hat and my sunglasses. So I walked to the end of the pier holding Billy's hand. I entered the bar; everyone stared. I asked the barman for a beer, he asked me what kind; I had no idea; so I just said, "Any kind". The barman then said, "ID please". I knew that at the base they always asked for ID, but I wondered why here. So I asked, "Why do you need my ID". "Madame, we need your ID". I answered, "Why do you need my military ID, we are not on the Base". He kindly said, "I need to see any ID to be sure that you are older than 21". I must have turned 100 colors. I showed him my ID, and he said, "Oh sorry, Madame". I took the beer, went back to Dave and said, "Don't you ever send me for a beer." I told Dave why, he thought it was funny, and I should take it as a compliment that I looked less than 21 years old.

I always looked young for my age. I remember that when we went to see the lawyer on the base to draw Dave's will, he asked Dave if I was his daughter. Dave got quite angry.

## South Carolina

We went to Shaw Air Force Base and we got housing on the base, a duplex. I did not work, since I was pregnant, but I did volunteer at the Thrift shop to help new coming military till I realized I was doing all the work while the officer's wives would be sitting around talking and drinking coffee, so I quit.

During my pregnancy, I had many problems. I became very anemic. The doctor prescribed iron pills. I started taking them but after one week I started itching all over my body. It went on for a week, finally I went back to the same doctor, and he told me that I was having a bad reaction to iron pills and I should stop taking them. I used to go to bed covered with Calamine lotion to ease the itching. Dave was gone most of the time during the 20 months that we spent at Shaw Air Force Base. When I went into labor, he was supposed to go to Washington. He deliberately missed the plane so he could stay with me. Bob became very sick when drinking baby milk; he had a bad reaction, so we were giving him Soy Bean milk, quite expensive.

I learned how to drive by myself, by practicing on the flight line, till the MP (Military Police) told me not to do it. I received my license, I scared the instructor; I was driving 10 miles below speed limit. I had put breaks on to stop so I would not hit a squirrel, and drove down the boulevard on the wrong side. I was not used to boulevards. He said, "Please drive faster". (He should see me now). In Italy to get a driver license is quite expensive and a long process, you must take two exams; one about car's engines, and how it works and then the driving test. Gas is also very expensive. (It is now in the U.S.)

Dave asked for a transfer to Italy, but he received Germany. I applied for my citizenship. Normally you have to wait three years to become a US citizen, but because Dave was going to Europe, they wanted to be sure that I went as an American citizen not as an Italian citizen in case of an emergency (cold war). I studied, went to Columbia. S.C. for my testing. During the test I got confused. The judge asked me, "Who is our Vice President." Instead of saying Hubert Humphrey, I said Humphrey Bogart. He laughed and gave me the Okay. It was quite a ceremony, but I was an American Citizen after only 20 months of being in the United States. Bob had been born 2 weeks before.

We had a dog, called Trista (in Italian it means sad, because of her drooping eyes). This dog did not like to stay inside the fence, so she would run away, and go to the flight line. The Flight Line Officer would call the house and say, "Sergeant Wills your dog is on the flight line again, come and get him". Dave would go, till the next day would happen again. We even tied her to the fence; she would break the rope and again go on the flight line. We finally gave her to someone that had a used car lot.

My mother, Bill and I went to a Kmart in Sumter, South Carolina. They had Blue Light specials. I had never been in a big store; in Italy we had small ones all over the city. When we walked in, we had a cultural shock. We had never seen so many Afro Americans in one place. We did not know what to do; we were the only white people in the store. But everyone was kind and polite, so we went on and shopped. It was quite an experience. (When I was a child, actually all Italian children, when they did not behave, the parent would say to them: "I am going to call the black man. (Uomo nero)")

Shaw Air Force Base was located in a beautiful wooded area, with a lake full of ducks and swans and we will go and feed them. Dave was gone so much that one day when he returned home and I opened the door, Bill said, "Mom, who is this man". I knew we had to leave South Carolina. His Commanding Officer loved to go in the field (I guess he hated his wife) and they will be gone for weeks, he even went to Puertorico for 3 weeks. Since I was pregnant, I spent most of my times watching TV, especially game shows, and my mother would watch soap operas, even if her English was limited. The lady across our duplex was German with two little girls. When we went to visit her, we had to take our shoes off and leave them outside; the house was spotless. We thought at that time how strange it was, but now in both my house and Marilou's house when we go in, we take our shoes off. She also cheated on her husband. When Dave and her husband were going in the field (they were both in the same unit), a young lieutenant will show up at her house and stay for hours. The husband finally found out and divorced her.

Since I was not working we had to watch what we spent. I bought a book on how to cook rice in 100 ways, and believe me I did cook that rice in 100 ways. My grocery bill for a week was $50.00 and at that time was quite high.

## From South Carolina Back to Germany

We could not take all our furniture with us, so we stored some in South Carolina. In Italy a friend of us (our neighbor) had given us a beautiful marble chess table. He told us that during World War II, his family had taken that chess table from the museum, and he was concerned in having it in the house, besides he did not play chess. So he had given it to Dave. The chess tabletop had black and white marble carved in, just gorgeous. We decided to store it in South Carolina. Unfortunately Dave made the mistake in telling the movers to be careful with that chess table, and how important it was. (He was a very trusting man). When we came back from Germany and had the furniture delivered to our Florida' address, the chess table was gone. We asked to be refunded the cost of the chess table about $2,000 (probably worth more than that, but we did not have a receipt). A young captain wrote us back telling us they would give us $100.00 and what was a Sergeant doing with a so expensive item anyway. I told him I will write to my senator, and he answered, "We have a storage place in the basement full of letters from Senators". I wrote to Senator Thornburg, the senator from South Carolina, and told him exactly what the Captain had said. We did get reimbursed; we do not know what happened to the Captain.

We arrived in Germany, it was in June and snowing. Our clothes had not arrived yet, so I took my two children and my mother and went to Italy to see my brother. Dave came after two weeks, saying he had found me a job as a bookkeeper on the base at the Rod and Gun Club and that our furniture and clothes were on the way. So we returned to Germany. We were living on the economy, since there was no housing available on base. The landlord' son wasn't very bright and his name was "Ano" which in Italian means butthole. We laughed every time his father called him. In the meantime they had closed Spangdhalem except for housing, and Dave had to drive to Bitburg.

Dave had to go back to the US on an emergency leave. I remained with my mother and Bill and Bob at Spangdhalem Air Force Base. Now we lived in housing (apartment building) second floor. We used to shop on the economy especially for meat, so every Saturday I drove my whole gang down to the city. One Saturday the two boys started arguing in the back seat. I parked, opened the door, told them to be quiet, and while closing the door, I did not pull my hand fast enough, and smashed my thumb. We went to the emergency room, I had a black thumb; I learned how to use the calculator with my left hand, I still do. I did not tell Dave till he returned; I did not want him to be worried.

I never had my ears pierced. In South Italy as soon as a little girl is born they pierce the ears. My mother thought that was barbaric, so I never had it done.

While in Germany, Dave promised me golden earring if I had them pierced. So, bravely (I hate needles) I went to the military hospital and asked the nurse to do it. Would you believe that my ears became infected? I would have been better off going to the German store to have it done. Anyway they healed, and Dave did buy me my first pair of earrings with 2 little diamonds.

While in Germany Bob was quite sick with his asthma, and we made many trips to the hospital, with worries.

We also purchased a collie (our first collie) on the German market. The dog (Lupo) became very sick, he had distemper, we cured him, and he was a good dog, even if not very smart. He loved putting his head outside the window of the car. One day we were driving away, dog's head sticking out, we were on base so Dave was not going very fast, all of the sudden, we heard a thump, Lupo had fallen from the car's window, he was not hurt, he just looked stupid. No more open windows for him. In the winter time when Dave and I were working and there was a lot of snow on the ground, and my mother with the two small children could not take Lupo out, she will put him outside on the balcony, he will lift his leg and do his business. There was lots of yellow snow.

Dave worked very hard in Germany. In 1969, he forgot our wedding anniversary. He had worked straight for 3 days . . . I was hurt, but I knew why. Every year I would say, "Remember when you forgot our anniversary?" . . . . and we would laugh about it.

## Some German Customs

In Germany they have what is called 'Fasching'. It takes place during the Mardi Gras. One year Dave dressed up as Caesar (Emperor of Rome)

and I dressed up as Cleopatra. We went to the NCO club and we won 1<sup>st</sup>
place, 5 bottles of champagne. It was fun.

At Christmas, Saint Nicholas would come to all the apartments, dressed as a bishop, with a chimney sweeper man, next to him, all dressed in black. You had to hire them. If you had been good you would receive candies otherwise coal. When Bob and Bill saw the Bishop and the man dressed in black, they ran away in their room and started crying. It took a while to get them to come out and talk with Saint Nicholas. At Christmas, Dave built a moveable Santa using a rotisserie for movement. It took the whole balcony. Everyone looked in awe. We took it back with us to Florida and used it for many years till it finally broke. Dave was very good with his hands, and in building and modifying things.

We had a German maid. She was very good in cleaning our apartment, and our refrigerator of beer. I was not home, my mother was, and could not do anything about (I guess that is where the Merry Maids started).

I worked on the Base as an accountant. Stephan (a German employee) was very ugly with everyone, and since Italians (actually no Europeans get along with the Germans, in fact one time we went to Italy in a rental car with German plates, we were lost and asked an old man for directions, he told us, "go home you Germans". When I explained it was a rental and I was Italian, he gave us all the directions that we needed) had never gone along with Germans, when I wanted to be really mean, I would sing 'Lilli Marlene', which is about a German prostitute during World War II. He used to get all red, and furious.

For Halloween in Germany, my mother and I made clothes for the children. It was snowing, and Bob was dressed as an Angel, but I did not want him to catch a cold (because of his asthma) so I made him wear cowboy boots. Every one kept saying, "I have never seen an Angel wearing cow boy boots". My mother also made for Bill and Bob a miniature Air Force uniform; they looked so cute in it. We used to dress them up in different costumes, Bill with a turban, Bob in other outfits and took pictures. We thought they were so cute.

# Trip to Berlin

In 1969 while we were in Germany, we decided to visit East Berlin, at that time separated from West Berlin by a wall. Since Dave worked in Intelligence he had to have special permission from his commander. Dave, Bill, Bob and I were able to travel on the military train; my mother had to take the German train. We left our different ways, and we decided to meet at the train station in West Berlin to pick my mother up.

Our voyage on the military train was quite spectacular, not comfortable, but as the train travelled thru the countryside we could see the Volpos (East Berlin guards) guarding the railroad with machine guns. We finally arrived, but there was no sign of my mother. We became worried, we sent someone to find out what was going on. Apparently my mother had gotten confused, and when the train had stopped at the station she had remained on the train, till she was in East Berlin. The train station was the same on both East and West side, you really couldn't tell in which part you were and the signs were all in German. My mother spoke fluent French but not German. When she got off the train, she did not see us, but just many armed guards, she was smart enough to stay in the station and not go outside, otherwise she would have been arrested and cause an International incident since she had a US military ID card. Dave changed in a civilian uniform, and then accompanied by two MPs went to East Berlin to pick her up. The American police did not talk with the East German policemen, since US did not recognize East Berlin. Finally he met my mother, while the children and I were waiting in a big square. It was quite a scare. We stayed at the hotel and then decided to visit East Berlin.

We boarded a U.S. military bus. At Checkpoint Charlie, the Volpos made us stay in the hot bus while they checked underneath the bus with mirrors, and all over to see if anyone was trying to enter the country. They were deliberately taking their time. I got mad, my children were hot and crying, and so I stepped out of the bus and told the Volpos: "It is hot inside the bus, I am staying outside". I don't think they had never had that happened. The children and I stayed outside in the shade of the trees; other American women followed my lead. The men stayed on the bus; they were wearing uniforms. Finally when the bus had been thoroughly checked we went back on, and continued our trip to East Berlin. We saw the bunker were presumably Hitler had died. It was quite interesting. People were very nice especially with the children. We also saw the changing of the guards, with the guards doing their famous goose steps.

We also approached the wall and saw many crosses. This was the place where the East Germans had tried to escape and the Volpos had shot them. There were houses cut in half, with half in East Berlin and half in West Berlin. The whole East Berlin looked very sad with unpaved streets. People looked very sad.

In West Berlin there was a half destroyed church as a reminder of the war. An American pilot had dropped a bomb on the church, children had been hiding in the church and they all died. The pilot did not know that it was a church, and did not know that there were children in the church. He was trying to get rid of the bombs before returning to the base.

# Camping with Dave, my Mother and Children in Naples, Italy

Dave had decided to go on a camping trip to Italy. As you know from before, I don't particularly like to go in the woods and I had never been camping. Dave rented two military tends. We had decided to go to Naples, at the outskirt of the city. We loaded our station wagon with all kinds of food and military issued food. The trip down was nice. We stopped at the campground in Pisa. Dave had a hard time setting up the tends. I was not much of help, but I tried. Dave did most of the cooking and the campground was full of Germans and British people and some Italians, but mostly Germans. We also took our dog "Lupo" with us. We did not want to leave him behind. I hated all the bugs, but we did meet a nice couple from Czechoslovakia. We talked about the oppression in their country, and they gave us for souvenir a glass pipe, which I still have. They had a gorgeous tend, looked like a miniature house with all the comforts. Our military tend paled in their comparison. We went to the military beach, visited my friends and spent two weeks. Then we returned to Germany. It was a memorable trip, certainly adventurous. Dave had been in the survival school during his military career and he knew all the plants and which ones to eat and not to eat. The children learned a lot, I did not particularly care to eat grass. During the night, Lupo would bark to anyone coming by. And it rained every single night. The children, my mother and Dave were fine and having fun, I was miserable.

## Other Trips

In 1968 we took a trip down to Italy, not camping this time. I was driving the station wagon; Dave, Bill, Bob and my mother were sleeping away. We were going down theAlps. A little Italian car passed me and blew the horn. At that time Italian men felt women did not belong behind a wheel. I stepped on the gas and passed him, and blew my horn; this went on for about 20 miles. Then he went his way waving and I waved back. Dave woke up and said, "Man, we are making good time". I told him the truth; he almost had a heart attack.

After Italy we went to Paris, France. Dave had parked the car in front of the hotel and checking for availability. I stayed in the car. All of the sudden something hit the back of the car, I went out and there is this guy, drunk, stumbling out of his car. I told him in French I was going to call the Gendarme, he begged not to. Since there was no damage to the car I let him go.

We also climbed the Eiffel Tower in Paris, the Arc de Triumph. We visited the Louvre. Very interesting was the Venus of Milo, the winged goddess and the Monna Lisa. I was disappointed in the Monna Lisa; I didn't realize it was not a huge painting. As a side trip we went to Versailles and saw the hall with 100 mirrors. (The queen of Austria was jealous of Versailles and they duplicated the hall of Mirrors in their royal palace, in Vienna).

We went many times to Luxembourg. At the Luxembourg train station I could purchase my Italian puzzle books. Across the train station there was a little Italian restaurant with very good food, and the shopping was much cheaper then in Germany. It was only 2 and half hour from Bitburg, so we took frequent weekend trips. (When we went back in 1990, with Marilou and my mother, we were able to visit the Cemetery, in Luxembourg, where General Patton' grave faces his soldier's burial site. It was quite impressive).

We took many trips to Holland. We took Bill and Bob to Madurodam (a little miniature city); we also took a boat ride and saw the house where Ann Frank had stayed during WWII in hiding. It was summer, but so cold; we went to the store and bought very heavy coats. Holland is famous for diamonds, coming from South Africa. We saw how they cut them. They must be cut with a precise hit, if the cut was not what they wanted, they would just throw the chips away. We also saw many windmills; they are there only as a tourist attractions, nowadays they are not used.

My mother used to take short trips to Italy to visit my brother. We would drive her with our little Volkswagen Beetle (we had paid $50 for it. We had purchased the car from another military person. You were allowed to bring your car overseas and they would ship it back to the States for free, but if you had purchased a foreign car, you had to pay for your own shipment, quite expensive, so many military personnel would sell their foreign made car cheaply.) On the way back from the train station the car engine went out. We slowly pushed it to the nearest gas station. It would have cost more than $50 to repair it and we were about to return to the

States, so we abandoned the car at the gas station and took a military bus back to the base.

When Dave retired we had decided to come to Florida. Before leaving Germany, everyone had to take a TB tine test. The military required a TB tine test instead of X-rays (cheaper). My test returned positive. Then I remembered that when I was young I had had pleura, so I asked the corpsman to just give me X-rays. He instead gave me another TB test (is a shot in the arm). I was worried that I had to remain behind and not being able to leave with Dave and my children. My arm became swollen. I was having a bad reaction. So this time Dave went to see the Base Commander and demanded X-rays. The chief doctor told us later that if I had received one more TB tine shot, I could have died from it. I was given X-rays and I did not have tuberculosis. I had promised my brother to see him before going back to the States. So my mother, Bill, Bob and I left on the train (Dave joined us later). I could not carry the suitcases because of the swollen arm, and a young man helped my family to get off the train. I was miserable with my arm hurting for almost a month. I cried when I left Italy, part of me was left behind, but my love for Dave and my children was stronger than my love for my country.

He retired just in time. His whole unit in Bitburg was sent to Vietnam and many died. Before that, when we left Shaw Air Force Base, his whole unit also went to Vietnam. Twice he escaped going to Vietnam. They offered Dave a chance to be promoted to Captain (by that time he had his B.A.), if he stayed an additional three years. I was tired of moving, it was very hard on the children. Dave decided not to accept and he retired. The last few months his uniforms were falling apart, but we did not buy any new ones since he was retiring anyway. We had decided to take Lupo with us. We had to pay $250.00 for his plane ticket, and then go to Atlanta, Georgia to pick him up. We called him the Golden Boy.

We arrived in New York. On the TWA plane they had given us apples to eat. While going thru customs, they told me I could not bring the apple in the US. I explained to the Custom agent, it was an American apple, from an American plane, to no avail. So I waited before going thru customs and finished my apple before entering the country. In Italy you don't throw away any food.

# Back to Florida

We arrived in Florida, with very little money. Dave retirement's check had not come in yet. We had to wait for another month. We did not have any money. We had always paid cash for everything; we had no credit card, so no credit. In Europe during these times, people always paid cash, no credit card, not even checks. My mother had saved some money and she gave it to us. I had paid her $50 a week to look after my children. She did not want the money, but I wanted for her to be able to buy her own things without asking us. Dave called his brother Ted and asked him for a loan of $200, so we could feed our children. Ted told us, "Sorry, cannot do, my wife Virginia said not to give any money to any of my relatives, no matter what." Dave tried to tell him it was only for a month, but the answer was still no. It took Dave and I years to forget and try to forgive. Finally a kind lady working for the credit union loaned us $200.00. We lived in an apartment that Tookie (Dave's sister) had found us, and next to us lived a prostitute. The apartment was full of palmetto bugs. I was terrified. To feed the children we would give them our food, then Dave and I will go fishing, and eat whatever we caught. If we did not catch any fish, we will just have a cup of coffee for the whole day. I went with Dave while he was job hunting (my mother stayed at the apartment with Bill and Bob). We had an old Country Squire station wagon, that when it rained, it would stop running and Dave had to open the hood and dry the inside. We always went thru Bunnell, and for odd reasons, every time we drove thru Bunnell it would rain. We had very hard times. Dave even applied in Georgia. The principal talked to Dave on the phone and asked him, "Are you black?" "No, sir, I am not". "Sorry, I cannot hire you; I have to meet my quota of black teachers." Dave was astonished. Dave did tell me that when he first went in the military they had separate bathroom and water fountains for white and black people. I could not believe it. Other principals would say, "We don't like the way retired military teach, they are too strict".

Finally Dave found a job teaching at Bushnell. (The principal was retired military).

We purchased our first home in Pine Hills in Bel Aire Woods with a VA loan with only $200 down. The home cost $33,000. At that time it was quite pricey. Because of the difference of our ages and we had small children, we tried to purchase Mortgage Insurance, which it would have paid the house off if either of us would die. We took a physical, and the doctor told Dave to stop smoking, his lungs were not in good shape. They sold us the insurance by combining our ages. Dave quit smoking cold turkey. It was hard; he gained 40 pounds and almost went back to smoking. But I nagged him not to go back to smoking. I took all the ashtrays away, I was a non-smoker, and it made it easier for Dave. Besides I was pregnant. We had never owned or lived in a big home before, we just loved it. David liked to use his hands and with my help, he build a chimney, changed the backyard, and then we had a pool put in. He planted grapes, he loved to grow vegetables, so did my mother, she had a green thumb, and so we had a vegetable garden. I don't have a green thumb. We had a little fence in the backyard. Lupo liked to jump the fence. One day we found him dead, we took him to the vet. His stomach had flipped and he had died. It was a very rare disease. Our golden boy had died, and the children were heartbroken. We purchased two collies and called them, Romeo and Juliet. Dave loved Shakespeare, and I loved Romeo and Juliet. We wanted more dogs, so we went to the Humane Society. There it was a beautiful German shepherd puppy. We took him home. One year later, his face was one of a German shepherd, but he had very short legs (like a basset hound). He was fierce, and barked to everyone. People would laugh, they would see this big head and short legs dog. Dave also changed the garage in a playroom, with a fireplace, a pool table, a piano and a TV, and closed up the entrance to the garage. Only drawback was that when we went food shopping (normally once a month), it was hard to carry the food upstairs.

Our neighbors were fine; we made friends with people across the street, Susan and Jerry and played bridge with them every Friday night. I was a lousy player but thank goodness Dave was good. Dave had learned how to play bridge when he was 10 years old. His mother was a fanatic bridge player, and she would meet with her friends to play every week. When she was short of a player she would use Dave. She taught him how to play at an early age. Dave was trying to write a book on an easy way to play bridge, but he never finished it.

One month our light bill came in. It was over $350.00. We were shocked. I was furious; I called Orlando Utilities, threatened them to go back to candles, and demanded for someone to check the meter. Someone did come; the meter had malfunctioned. They adjusted our bill and replaced the meter. From then on I kept track of the reading.

I started having some strange dreams. I would be in a castle, and I couldn't find my way out. I would run, run and cry. Dave would gently touch my shoulder, trying to wake me up, when he would hear me whimpering. I had this same dream for many years and then the dream stopped. I don't know why it started and why it stopped. But I was glad that it stopped, because it was terrifying.

I found a job at American Cryogenics, downtown Orlando, and then I became pregnant. First I cried because the boss told me I could not return to work after the birth of the child and we needed the money so badly. Then when Marilou was born (as Dave used to say the first girl in 50 years), everything was wonderful. He purchased cigars for every staff member at the school and candies for all his students. He was the happiest man on earth. 'His pupi' as he called Marilou was his proud and joy. I was also the happiest mom on earth. I always wanted a little girl, I never had a sister, and I thought it would be great to share things and have her as a friend when she got older. My mother was also happy; she told me, "This baby will always bring you happiness". We planted a tree in the front of our house when she was born (the tree is still there).

While I was pregnant, my mother and the boys and I had gone shopping. On the way home (I was driving the station wagon) on highway

50, I could see from the rear mirror that the car coming behind me was not going to stop. I was at a red light and I had no place to go. I pressed on the brakes really hard and told my mother and the children to hold on because he was going to hit us. Then the car hit us. At that time only drivers had seat belt, Bill and Bob were sitting in the back and they got thrown around. The other driver's car radiator was destroyed; my car only had a small dent. Trooper Lane (our neighbor), came, and they arrested him on the spot (he was trying to bribe the trooper, he was drunk). I had never seen anyone searched and handcuffed before except in the movies. The insurance man kept the file open till Marilou was born, to be sure that the baby was okay. Dave, my mother and I were so worried, but everything came out all right.

Marilou was born on what used to be the naval base. We were living quite a distance from the hospital, so when I felt contractions, I told Dave it was time to go. We arrived to the hospital, the nurse said, "not time yet, false alarm, go home". I didn't think she was right so I told Dave to just stay in the waiting room a little longer. After half an hour the nurse passed by and said "are you still here?" I said, "Yes, my contractions are 5 minutes apart". Her face got white, they wheeled me in and Marilou was born.

The women all shared a big room separated just by curtains, certainly no privacy. In the morning we will get up and pick up our baby from the nursery. Marilou was the only white female baby in the nursery and the nurses had placed a pink ribbon on her head. One day I approached the nurse to get my baby. She handed me a little Afro American boy. As politely as I could, I said, "This is not my baby, I have a girl". The boy's mother was behind me and she was extremely insulted by the situation. When Marilou misbehaved, we would say, "Did they switch our baby?" She was the prettiest in the entire nursery; even the doctor said so. We took many pictures of Marilou; she looked like Bill when he was a baby, even her personality and her behavior. She was an exact clone. She adored her big brother and tried to copy him in many ways. Unfortunately due to the lack of money, after two weeks, I was looking for a job. It was hard to feed six people, but our kids never lacked anything. I found work at

Southern Gold (I had to sit on a cushion I was still so sore) an Orange Juice company, at a $2.25 an hour. I used to skip lunch so I could get overtime. I had no idea of what happened to oranges after they had been picked, but I learned fast and eventually became the Comptroller of the company, and an expert in Drawback customs. The Personnel Officer, Mr. Harrison, (his wife had made dresses for the dolls in the "It's a small world" ride at Disney World) that hired me had been in the military and understood the situation. One strange custom the business had was that when they decided to fire someone, they would take him/her to lunch, pay for the lunch and give him/her the severance check. We never saw the person come back to work again. I was the only one to know, because I was the payroll clerk and I had to prepare their severance check.

Southern Gold was pretty close to our house. It took only 15 minutes to get to work. One day while driving, the car slid and made a 360-degree turn. There was an oil spot in the street. I stopped inches from the electrical pole; I was shacking so badly, it took me almost twenty minutes before I could actually start driving again. When I arrived at work I was still shaken, I called my mom to tell her, I could not call Dave because he was in the classroom.

I was a pretty woman. One supervisor used to call me Babe, Honey and so one. These terms were quite irritating. I would ask him to stop doing it, but he completely ignored me. So one day while he was walking with all his employees around him I said, "Hey Babe, how are you. Here boy take this paperwork". His face turned red, and from then on he either called me Ms. Rose or Ms. Wills.

My best friend was Ruby and Bobbie Green. Bobbie had taught me everything about the computer, an old one that used cassette tapes to store information. She used to look after our pets when we went vacationing. She left for Missoula, Montana and I took her job. We used to play on the radio station, WKIS, to win prizes or money while we were working. I don't know what happened to her.

We were on the 2<sup>nd</sup> floor and the outside steps had a red light on the door. We used to laugh about "we look like a red light district." We were in Pine Hills and one time a guy driving a Cadillac hit the fence, cops had pursued him, he was carrying drugs.

It was an old building. One time I went to work and the room smelled horribly. A rat had fallen between the two walls, he had died and smelled and could not be removed. The smell lasted for a month.

One of the employees, Roger McKibben, used to tell us that when he went to college he was poor, that he ate many times dog biscuits. He said they were pretty good. He married our receptionist.

The Company had been held from the same owners for many years. The owners decided to sell it to Ventura Company, in California, which was in turn owned by 7Up, which was in turn owned by Philip Morris. The Comptroller, Harold Knott, had been asked to leave, and I was now the Comptroller of the Company. They hired a new guy, Bob Keyes, and the president of the company, George Nagel, told me that I would now be Assistant Comptroller, a demotion in my eyes. I told him not to do it, but he did not comply. So I wrote to Mr. Weissman, the president and CEO of Philip Morris, explaining the situation, and my feelings that the only reason I had been demoted was because I was a female, and foreign born. Mr. Weissman told the president to reinstate me as a Comptroller and make the other person Vice President of Finance. For a year I was making more money than he was. It was a personal satisfaction.

Being an orange juice company, in the summer we had nothing to do. When the lawyers from Philip Morris would come down to check our records, we will cover our desk with papers so that we looked busy. I was in college and I was able to study at my desk.

Our son Bob loved animals so he would come home with strained cats. One time in the winter, it was quite cold, I started my car to go to work and I heard a 'miao' coming from under the hood. Dave came, opened the hood, and three cats jumped out (they were staying on top of the engine to keep warm). We also had a turtle, Teresa. Dave's teacher friend had asked Dave to watch after her Saint Bernard, Cuddles, for a few days. He was a huge dog. Marilou loved to sit on him, as he was a horse. Cuddles did not like it. Cuddles was territorial and he got rid of our turtle, we only found the shell. We told Marilou that the turtle had decided to move away with another shell. She believed us, she was only 5 years old. Cuddles used to scare our garbage man and our postman by standing up at the gate with his big head and roughly barking. One day I found Cuddles laying on the steps, inside the house, he had died of a heart attack. I had to call the Humane Society to come and help move him; he was so big and heavy. That day we all cried.

At Easter we bought 3 baby chicks, they told us they would die, but they didn't, we had 2 chickens and one rooster. The chickens laid eggs, but the rooster was too noisy. Our neighbors complained and we had to get rid of them. My mother killed them but we could not eat them, they were our pets.

Out of our two collies Romeo and Juliet, Juliet was the smart one. She was allowed to stay in the house, and she would sleep by Marilou's bed and if Marilou started to cry, she would come and start barking at us. We were treating both dogs with heartworm pills. These worms could eventually kill the dogs unless they took these pills. We went for a trip and left the two dogs with our veterinarian. When we came back, Juliet had died. They had given her by mistake a double dose of heartworm pills. Dave had to dispose of Juliet and he cried all the way to the vet and back. We all cried. She was the best dog we had never had.

When Marilou was 5 years old she did not like to wear clothes. So she would strip and run around the house naked. One day a teacher, Dave's friend had stopped by. From the corner of my eye I could see that Marilou had stripped and was about to run in the living room. I ran to her, grab her before anyone would notice and took her in her room and put on her a bathing suit, which she could not take off. All thru the summer she wore that bathing suit.

When Bob was a small child he had the bad habit to put things in his mouth. We kept warning him about the danger, but to not avail. One day we were driving down Old Winter Garden Road, Bob, Bill and my mother were sitting in the back seat. Dave was driving. All of the sudden we heard Bob scream. Dave stopped the car on the side of the road, I turned around, Bob had a penny stuck between his front teeth and couldn't pull it out. I leaned backwards and slowly removed it, while tears kept flowing from Bob's eyes. That scared him so much that he never put any more objects in his mouth.

Bill went to school, Bob was at home with my mother and Marilou and he really helped my mother by bringing baby bottles and other things. He was really good with Marilou. My mother had taken very good care of all my children. I couldn't have left them with a babysitter and going to work and not worry.

Bob also liked snakes, so we purchased three snakes (we actually paid for snakes); one ran away (we could never find it), two drowned when it rained. They were in an outside aquarium (Bob had forgotten to put the top on the aquarium). Also Bob had a cat, Fifi, and he had decided to toilet train her, he would sit that poor cat on the toilet when he thought it was time, and that poor cat never went. Bill was more in computers. Every Saturday Bill and I would go to a nearby elementary school (we had made previous arrangements with the principal) and he wrote computer math programs for elementary students. Thinking about now, we should have patented these programs.

Dave loved flowers and stones. On the way to Bushnell he always stopped to pick up big stones to place in our garden. He also made a sandbox for the children to play.

I had purchased a book on home decorations, and I decided to paint each door of a different color. The bathroom doors red (for emergency), bedroom door blue for the boys, and pink for Marilou and so on. Dave loved to wallpaper, he had done that with maps when he was in the military and he wallpapered Marilou's room, and the kitchen. Dave did a really good job.

Every Saturday we would go to Red Lobster with all the family, they had all you can eat shrimp, and we all loved shrimp. We used to call Bob the garbage disposal. When there was food left on the table he will say, "Give it to me. I'll finish it." It was a pleasure.

Bill and Bob were very easy to buy clothes for. Bob liked all clothes in blue and Bill liked them in brown. We used to go shopping at Montgomery Ward. Upstairs in the store they had live animals, and we would always go upstairs to look at them. There was a small monkey, and Dave decided to touch the monkey, and the monkey bit him. Blood everywhere, we were worried about rabies, but the store assured us that the monkey had been vaccinated. Dave always touched animals. He loved animals and they loved him. In one of our trips we went to Texas, saw the Alamo and Saint Antonio, then decided to go across the border to Mexico. Bill had to go to the bathroom; we stopped at one of the stores, and asked permission to take Bill in the back to use the restroom. I took Bill to the restroom. Dave stayed in the front with the rest of the family. There was a dog in the front of the store and Dave started to pet him. The dog bit him; we had to go to the American Hospital, to be sure that the dog did not have rabies. The military doctors checked out and he told us that all dogs in Mexico were vaccinated against rabies. It was the law. Dave had told me that when he was young, a squirrel had bitten his finger while he was trying to feed him.

When we went to Reno, Nevada, they had slot machines everywhere. I am not a big gambler, so when I played the 5 cents machine and won, I kept my 10 dollars. I also played the penny machine; Marilou was outside with Dave and the rest of the family, as soon as I won two dollars, I quit and gave the money to Marilou.

While Bill and Bob were quite easy to go shopping for, Marilou on the other hand was very hard to please. One time we entered a shoe shop, she tried every shoe in the store, and then she decided she didn't like any of them. Dave and I used to draw straws to see who would take her shopping. I ended up loosing all the times. I think Dave cheated.

Bill and Bob were quite a handful. Our home at Peachwood Lane was a split-level house. One day we were all upstairs except for the boys who were downstairs in their room. We thought they were too quiet; we walked downstairs. They had taken a battery apart to see what was inside, and they ruined the brand new carpet. I could have died. Dave said, "What an inquisitive mind, they are so smart."

Dave loved fishes, so downstairs we had two big aquariums, one for fresh water fish and the other one for salt-water fish. We used to go fishing and if we caught one still alive, we will place it in our aquarium. We caught a sailing cat fish one time that ate meat, so we would feed him little pieces of hamburger meat everyday.

Many times when we went fishing, some members of the family will leave the front door unlocked. We would come home and blame whoever was the last one to leave the house (normally Dave). Now even when I cut the grass I lock the front door. Times have certainly changed.

One year we had a bad hurricane "David", and the whole family, including the dogs slept downstairs in the family room. It was quite a scare; I had never been in a hurricane before. We did not suffer any damage, except the cover of our boat blew away.

Bob's asthma was not any better. One time we had to take him to the military hospital on emergency, and they gave him the wrong dose of medications, causing him to get worse. We yelled for hours to the doctor.

When Bill was young he ate his meat almost raw, that Nonna would fix for him. A couple years later he decided that he wanted very well cooked meat, almost burned. I guess his body was requiring different taste of meat.

Bob and Bill were heavy sleepers. Dave would leave around 06:30 AM for work, I much later, so in spite of the alarms, I would go downstairs and say, "Bill, Bob, time to get up". Ten minutes later back downstairs. One day I was so angry, it was my 5th trip downstairs; I poured some water on both Bill and Bob. From then on they woke up on time.

While shopping at the Navy Base, we had met two Italian sailors, Franco and Pio. We made friends with them. They helped us concrete our patio in the back yard; we had them for dinner everyday. When they left I was very sad, we wrote for a while but slowly we drifted apart. One bad accident happened at Thanksgiving. Franco and Pio were at our house for the feast. I was about to take the turkey out of the oven and I did not see that Marilou was behind me, I ran into her, hot oil splashed out. She started crying. I was screaming. Dave and I took her right the way to the Mercy Hospital emergency room. She was okay; it was a scare. It was a Thanksgiving that we would never forget. (Yes, I did cook every Thanksgiving, Christmas, Easter and so on. I cook well; it is just not my favorite thing to do).

We had a large pool installed, with a diving board and a slide. We wanted a Solar Heater so we could swim year around. It was expensive, so Dave went to the library, got some books, and he build the solar panels for our pool. The solar panels worked very well. He dreamed to attach our water heater to it, but we never did. My mother and I paid $50 each to Marilou if she would jump from the diving board and she did. The boy went to YMCA to learn how to swim, and they taught Marilou.

The house was 75 miles away from Bushnell. Dave put almost 45,000 miles on his brand new car in a year. In the night Dave went to UCF to work on his Master's degree. He was having trouble with one professor about a thesis, so he went to Rollins College and finished his Master. Later he moved from Sumter High School (Bushnell), to Robinswood Junior High. The school was right behind our house. He did not particularly like teaching Middle School, so he got a job at Evans High after one year.

While at Bushnell, he was also a football coach, to get additional money ($300 a year). He was making around $5,000 a year when he first started teaching. They used to have alligators running on the football field. One of his friends told him, not to be afraid, if he saw an alligator, just to try to keep his mouth shut and poke a finger in his eye. I told Dave, "Don't you even think about it, run away from the alligator." They used to have at the end of the school year a picnic with all the staff. Good steaks but it was next to a cow pastures with flies all around.

Dave was a good man, (when he left the military, they gave him a plaque saying "The Last of the Good Guys" and he loved it) and he used to give rides to hitchhikers. I kept telling him how dangerous it was, but he used to say he had hitchhiked many times when he was in the military and everyone always stopped. He stopped doing that when one of his student's father had been killed by a hitchhiker. He understood how dangerous it had become. It was sad.

The Hiawassee Elementary School was few blocks from our house. My mother would walk the children there and later she will wait at the corner for them. The children, especially Marilou, would call me when they got home. Marilou always complaining, "Bill and Bob are picking on me." I would talk to the boys and they would quiet down. That went on every day. Marilou loved talking on the phone. Dave and I thought that she would become a telephone operator. She also could not keep any secrets. We called her the 'informer'.

Marilou and I decided to exercise so we will walk (when I came from work), from our house all the way up to Hiawassee road. At the end of the road there was a Carvel ice cream store. We will stop there and have a nice ice cream or shake, and then walk back down to the house. We did not loose any weight but we had fun.

When Dave was teaching, teachers were allowed to paddle their students if they misbehaved. Dave had made a paddle for the occasion (I still have it). He did not paddle hard and the students were allowed to sign the paddle afterwards. They all tried to be paddled so that they could sign it.

For our anniversary Dave and I had decided to go to Tampa for one day and stay overnight. We had never gone away by our self; we did go every Friday to supper and a movie, (Dave was always working at two jobs and working long hours, I felt he deserved it), but trips wise we went always as a family. (By family I mean all of us and my mother, she was part of our family, extended family but still family). We left Bill, Bob and Marilou with my mother. We came back on Sunday; Dave went to work on Monday. When he walked in the school one of his friend teachers asked him, "Are you all right, did you and Rose were able to post bail, what happened?" Dave had no idea of what he was talking about. So he finally said, "What is going on."? His friend said, "I called home on Saturday and the answering machine said, "my mom and dad are in jail, and they are trying to post bail, I'm here all by myself, bye." Dave was furious. When he came home we listened to the answering machine, it was Bob's voice. He thought that was very funny. He has always been a joker. We did not think it was funny at that time, and then later (many years later) we laughed about. The same Bob, the joker, for Halloween one time, used all Dave's wood, to make a casket, where he would lay in it, and then jump up and scare the kids. Les (his friend) and Bob both built the casket.

Sea World owned Florida Festival, and for Halloween they had a competition for best costumes. Bob and Bill built a huge shark; at that time the film 'Jaw' was quite popular. He lost to 'Dart Vader', but the costume was beautiful. Marilou went as a belly dancer (wearing one of her ballet costumes). At the restaurant at Florida Festival they used to serve alligator's tail, we never touched it.

Dave was a great teacher, everyone at Evans High School loved him, and years later, if some of his past students would see him they would make a point to come, thank him and the girls hug him. He was a generous man, and if a student needed lunch money, he would give to them. If another teacher asked for money he would do the same thing. He also did that while in the military. I used to get upset with him, because money was tight, and these people never returned the money, but he just could not say "no".

He would help anyone. Bob is the same as David. Many times Bob would go helping perfect strangers and also his friends to move furniture, paint, or work in the yard.

Bob was always thinking outside the box. I used to collect coins, and couldn't understand why they kept disappearing, till one day Bill told me that Bob had been used these coins to buy lunch. He still denies it.

# Family Trips

While working for Southern Gold, in the summer I had 4 weeks off, so Dave, the children and my mother would take long trips throughout the Unites States. During the trip Bill and Bob will misbehave in the car, normally picking on Marilou, who sat in the front seat. We would promise that when we got home they would receive licks with the paddle. One time we were up to 300 licks. We never followed thru with our threats.

We used to go to Battle Fields (Dave was a super historian). One time we went to Tennessee and we were supposed to walk around the battlefield. The children and my mother and I were all walking behind Dave. It got dark we got lost. Bill was afraid that alligators would show up, so he stood behind us. Finally we saw a ranger (he was looking for us) and he took us back to the front gate. It was quite an experience.

We also went to the Grand Canyon and Petrified Forest. We had a Buick station wagon that used to heat up all the times (a lemon car). So while traveling thru the desert, the radiator hose gave up again. Dave went underneath, trying to patch the hose. The kids were playing in the hot sun, no one stopped to help us. We finally went on and had the car fixed at the garage.

I had just taken a course in Beat generation literature at Rollins College, and the teacher (which was later fired), had taught us how to chant (I had no idea what we were saying, but it did relax us). Some shri krisma followers (at that time very popular) approached us at the Grand Canyon, asking for money. I responded, "do you want to hear my chant?". They walked away. I used to keep the kids quiet by saying, "if you don't stop, I will start chanting."

When I get very nervous, even now I calm myself down by chanting. It works. I need to find someone from India to tell me what on earth I'm saying.

Shri krisna govinda

Are nurare

Hey nada nara,

Yana vasudeva

Hey nada nara yana vasudeva

Hey nada nara yana vasudeva

Shri krisna govinda

Only recently I went on google and find out that these words were in veneration of the Goddess Shiva.

We tried to save money during these trips, so we used to eat at truck stops. Bill always had a fit, and one day he refused to go in and eat, because it was a truck stop, (we used to call Bill the 'Duke'). We were in Tennessee, and when we left, the waiter said, "You'll come back, you hear". Marilou said to me, "Mom he is talking like the bear". I started laughing and took Marilou away. At Magic Kingdom there is a ride, 'Country Bear Jamboree' and at the end the bear says, "You'll come back, you hear." We thought it was very funny.

We also took a trip to Virginia; we had purchased a 24-foot camper trailer. We saw Niagara's falls. We could not stay in the town very long; the smog was so bad Dave could barely breathe. We went on the Canadian's side to see the falls. They were just gorgeous. We had taken the children and my mom all over the United States; see all historical sights, except Alaska and Hawaii. I was a member of the Smithsonian Institute, so we went to Washington quite often, and we ate at the Smithsonian. We also visited the FBI headquarters, and they showed us how they trained the agents. It was very interesting and definitely educational.

We used to go fishing every Saturday at Cocoa Beach, first by sitting on the bridge, and then with a small boat. Later on we purchased a 24-foot Cabin Cruiser, so it had a toilet that Marilou could use. Dave had a hard time docking the boat, he always slammed it against the pier, and the boys would pick on him. We had fun. The famous station wagon will heat up and one day we were stranded and had to call our friend, Slim Fender, to take us back home. We finally traded the car in for another car and sworn never to buy another Buick again and we didn't.

We went with two cars to Key West. Dave was pulling the boat, while I was following. Dave and I slept in the boat, the children and my mother in the camping ground cabins. The ocean was very rough; Dave was sleeping away. I woke him up and said, "Dave, the lamp post is moving." A hurricane was on the way. So we packed up the children, the car and headed back to Orlando. It was a rough drive, the wind was very strong and we even lost our license plate.

Bob and my mother had gone to Italy to see my brother. We had just driven them to 'La Guardia Airport'. Dave, Bill, Marilou and I decided to take a trip to Canada. While in Canada we visited an Atomic Power Plant. Marilou was not allowed in because of radiation, she was 9 years old, and so she stayed in the playing area. The rest of us went and stood on top of a reactor, a very interesting experience. While traveling in Canada, Bill was dying to go to the bathroom; we stopped at one of the farms, and asked them if he could use the bathroom. They pointed somewhere in the back, we stayed by the car. We waited for a while, no Bill, so we started walking towards the back of the farm, and calling, "Bill, Bill, where are you?". A tiny voice answered, "here, in this building". It was an outhouse; we had never seen an outhouse before, only Dave had. We laughed and finally Bill came out and we left. He was so embarrassed. Then Marilou had to go, so this time we stopped at a park, again outhouse with a hole in the ground. Marilou had a hard time going in it. She used to grade bathrooms according to a scale that she had made up, from 1 to 10; the outhouse was definitely in her opinion a 1. We went to Quebec. They spoke French and I felt very comfortable in re-using my French. Canada was gorgeous, with forests and so many friendly people.

Bill was 16, he had a permit to drive, but his behavior was so terrible, that we did not make him drive. He was having his usual temper tantrum. No idea why. We picked my mother and Bob up from La Guardia airport. I was so angry that I drove straight home for 22 hours.

# Dave also a Joker

When we went to restaurants, Dave had taught Bill and Bob a trick. You could fill the glass with water, put a paper towel on top of it, and carefully tip it over. When the waitress would come to clean up, and pick up the glass, the water would run all over the table. He also used to amuse the children by making a bra with the napkin. Marilou always laughed when he did this. (I called them rabbit ears)

When Marilou went to the orthodontist, Dr. Rubenstein, Dave would take her, then after the visit, he would buy her a coke float. Marilou did not like them and kept leaving them untouched, and Dave kept on buying them. He told me he was hoping that eventually she would like them. The orthodontist told us that her wisdom teeth needed to be pulled out. The first time we went to the surgeon, Marilou chickened out, and we left, the second time she finally had it done. She was under heavy sedition; Dave had to carry her upstairs in the bedroom. It was quite a job, especially with his bad back.

At Christmas all three children received an equal amount of money for toys. I was receiving a bonus from Southern Gold; some went in my retirement account (they did not have a pension plan) and the rest to buy toys for the children. We would buy individual toys for each one of the children and some toys that they could share.

During the summer we had annual passes to Sea World and later to Disney World. My mother and the three children will go to Sea World on Sunday, while Dave and I studied at home. Bill and Bob spent most of their times petting the dolphins.

Bill was a good bowler, and when he was 10 years old he won a bowling tournament and won a turkey for Thanksgiving. He wanted to be a pro-bowler; he also wanted to be an astral navigator.

All of our three children went to St. Andrews, and St. Charles and then Bishop Moore. The main reason was, one day while taking a trip, we asked Marilou to read a sign (she was in 2nd grade) and she could not. They were teaching her by memorizing words. Also one of Bill's teachers at Hiawassee Elementary had told Bill he had a big head. We went to see the principal, we were very angry. The teacher apologized. The next year we pulled the children out of the public school and placed them in private schools. It was expensive, but worth it. I would take them to school and Dave would pick them up. Except one day, Bill called from school and said, "Mamma, papa is not here." I called home; he was at home, sleeping. He had forgotten to pick them up, and he was so tired. (He had to get up very early in the morning to go teach to the High School). He left and went to pick them up. We never let him forget it, jokingly. Later on Bill would drive the children to school, but when he graduated, Bob was in charge, and he thought it was funny when everyday he would hit the fence at the school, and the principal would call us. Bill skipped school one time by staying home. The principal called me at work and wondered what had happened.

(It was never proven. Bob had a show and tell project; he brought to school the Tower of Pisa. The tower of Pisa came back broken . . . Who did it . . . till now the mystery remains . . . later on when Bob went to Italy he brought me back the Tower of Pisa . . . was it guilt . . . try to redeem himself . . . we don't know . . . the mystery continues . . .).

# First Trip to Europe

For Marilou's graduation from High School, we took her to Europe, the first time for 45 days. We took a military flight from Dover Air Force Base. Dave was allowed to do so since he was retired military. Marilou was on cloud nine. She was beautiful and all the airmen flirted with her. We landed in Spain. Since they used to call me a hermit, I stayed with the luggage and my mother and sent Dave and Marilou to rent a car. They came back all excited, Dave told me he had gotten a real good deal. Of course I should have gone since I spoke Spanish and they did not. Anyway we started driving; we went to Paris, France. Marilou loved Paris; she wanted to move there. We saw La Bastille (French prison), Versailles (the royal castle with the hall of 100 mirrors). We saw the Louvre. One day Dave went to get the car from parking, and Marilou and I were standing in the street. A man got out of this very expensive car, and approached us. I speak French so I could talk to him. He said, "I love your daughter's hair; she is so pretty, I like to have her in my commercials". I knew it was a scam. I said no thanks; we are leaving for the US in the morning. He kept insisting, and finally I told him if he did not go away I would call a gendarme (Europeans are very afraid of the police). He finally left. Marilou asked me what he wanted, when I told her the whole story, she thought she should have gone for it. Later we read in the paper that many girls had been abducted with excuses of stardom, and sold to Arabian Countries as slaves. In Paris we arrived on the 14th of July, Bastille Day. Big National Holiday, no a single restaurant was open except for a McDonald. We also found a gas station open that had food. Before we left beautiful Paris we stopped at one of the restaurant. We sat and noticed that a roach was crawling on our table (we were eating outside). Marilou called the waiter, the waiter came and said, ""Hu la la" and shooed the roach off our table and then said, "What would you like to eat."

After Paris we went to Switzerland, then Italy. I took her to see the house where I was born, and Nonna's house (in Lucca we entered the house where my mother was born and start taking pictures. Tourists thought that it must have been something historical and they also started taking pictures. It was quite funny) and the famous tower of Pisa. When we arrived at Pisa, Dave (due to his COPD) could not go up, so Marilou and I decided to walk up to the tower, while Dave was filming us. It was quite hard, since all the stairs were made of marble. We finally made it to the top, and waved down to Dave. Then we walked all the way down, out of breath. We wanted to see what we looked like, but Dave had not realized that the battery was not working, so nothing came out. There was no way that we would walk back up these stairs. Then we went to Rome, the Vatican City. Marilou decided to go shopping. We bought a beautiful dress for her prom, and then she decided to buy a bathing suit for $500.00, with a shawl. The funny thing was that the bathing suit had to be dry-cleaned. She wore it, but she never went into the water. We stayed at Camp Darby, an army base. Every day at 6:00 A.M. we were awaken by the Reveille. It made it hard to sleep, but it was cheap to stay.

In Florence, we were trying to find a parking place for our hotel the 'Caravel'. All the roads were (still are) one way, and we kept driving around and around. Finally we spotted a parking place right next to the train station in front of the hotel, Marilou jumped out of the car, and stood in the parking place, holding it for us. We drove around one more time, while Marilou kept shooing the other cars away. We finally parked. I don't think that would have worked in the States.

While driving we used to buy fresh fruit. I will be sitting in the back seat while they took turns driving. One time we purchased a box of grapes, and they placed it in the back seat. Dave and Marilou were talking away; finally Marilou turned around and said, "Why are you being so quiet." I had finished the whole box of grapes. I love fruit. They never let me take fruit in the back seat for the rest of the trip.

After Rome we went to Salerno to see my friend Rosetta, her husband Franco and her two grown children, Maurizio and Marcello. Marcello was horrible. We stayed at her house, and he locked us in the bathroom. We were about to kill him. With Rosetta and her family we took a short trip outside Salerno. We climbed a mountain; we stopped at a restaurant. Marcello wanted rabbit. The restaurant did not have it and so he had a temper tantrum. Then we decided to have the children ride horses. Marilou loved it. Marcello of course was having again a temper tantrum, he started running around the field, and he fell right in horse manure. He smelled all the way home. We tried not to laugh, (thank goodness we had our own car) but later we did say, "There is a God, justice has been made". Later on Marilou told me that Rosetta other son Maurizio, was trying to hook up with her. His mother would have loved if they got married.

We also stopped at Pilsen, in Czechoslovakia. We stayed in a run down hotel. Marilou was convinced that the owner was a vampire, there were no mirrors in the hallways and we only saw the owner at night.

When we went to Czechoslovakia, we went into a restaurant. Dave was trying to speak German with the waiter. The waiter brought the menu; it seemed pretty high in pricing. So Dave told me in English, "this is quite expensive". The waiter asked, "Are you Americans?" we answered, "Yes, we are." The waiter took our menu, came back with a different one, and said, "Americans are our friends". The items on the menu were much cheaper. In Salzburg, Austria we saw Mozart house. Marilou loved Mozart's music. We also went into a little chapel in Oberndorf where 2 friars had written "Silent Natch" (Silent Night). It was so peacefully. From downtown we also saw the castle where the Sound of Music had been filmed. Austrians are very friendly people, we were lost downtown, we stopped to ask a gentleman for directions and since his English was poor, he said, "Follow me, I'll take you there". What a nice gesture.

In Germany, we went to Dachau to see the concentration camp and the famous gas showers. It was quite impressive. Dachau was right in the middle of the town, and there was no way that the people in the village did not know what was going on behind these gates. When we went to Germany we could find no one that would say he was a Nazi, or had belonged to the Nazi party, even the older people would deny.

While in Europe we went thru Cannes. I knew that on the Riviera there was topless swimming. So I told Dave I was tired and he should be driving. He did, as we came by the Riviera, Marilou and I could see all kinds of girls on the beach topless. Dave kept saying, "Is that the reason I am driving, so I don't look?" We just laughed.

We went to Amsterdam. We had decided to stay in Utrecht. When we entered the hotel's elevator, Marilou noticed that the whole inside was full of graffiti. We were all shocked. Marilou said: "Look at the graffiti. I don't think I want to stay in this hotel." So I told her, "Let's wait and see and talk with the manager." When we arrived at the desk, we asked the manager, "Have you noticed that the elevator's walls are full of graffiti?" He looked at us with a puzzled look and said: "Yes, we have", and kept on filling up papers. We thought perhaps he did not understand us. Anyway we stayed. The hotel was pretty nice and clean. We left the next day, still puzzled. As we were driving, we noticed that all the bridges, walls and buildings were full of graffiti. Apparently there is nothing wrong with graffiti in Holland. Beautiful graffiti I would say. Now we understood the puzzle look on the manager's face. We visited the red light district; the whole town was very hippy. Holland is a free spirited country; it was a good experience.

We also went to London, and we stayed at Windsor, at the Christopher Wren's hotel. Again this hotel was supposed to be haunted by ghosts. Scaring was the driver, driving on the left side of the street, very scary. We visited the castle, and fed the pretty swans.

We made back to Spain to catch our flight back home (we were using military plane). Again I stayed at the airport with the luggage and Dave and Marilou took the car back. They brought the bill; I did not look at the bill. Going thru the military customs, we had a bottle of water. The MP took the bottle, shook it. We asked him why. He said, that many people would smuggle diamonds by placing them in a bottle of clear water, and unless you shook the bottle you could not see them. On the way to the States, the pilots had Marilou stay in the cockpit and when they approached Canada, talk on the radio with the Air Controllers. She was very excited. When we arrived home, days later the bill came from American Express and the rental car charge was $3,000. We could have purchased a new car in Spain for that price. Thank goodness I had charged it to American Express. American Express does not pay the business till they receive the money. I protested the bill. Dave had misunderstood between pesetas and American dollars. I paid only what I thought would have been a fair price. American Express had sent them a rebuttal letter. They had 30 days to answer to the American Express request, but their answer arrived on the 31st day, so we did not have to pay the $3000. It was my fault I should have gone instead of sending two people that did not speak the language. But it was a wonderful trip, expensive trip, over $30,000 dollars. I am sure a great experience for Marilou.

# Port Orange

We decided to buy some land. We looked everywhere, including Lake Mary, but finally we purchased 2 acres in Port Orange. We cleaned it all by our self, by borrowing a bobcat from Southern Gold. We went every weekend. Bob helped, Bill was always busy, and so he only helped sometimes. Marilou came but she would lay on top of the car and take suntan. We decided to build a log home, we got all the plans, and the logs from Tennessee, but the salesman did not help us at all. We made a lot of mistakes while building it that we tried to correct. Our only regret was that we had decided on a two stories house, it would have been much easier if it had been one story. We also found out that when it rained the place would flood, so we had to build the house on a higher ground. It took us two years, a lot of backbreaking, but we were proud. We also said never again.

One day Bob was with us, we were eating our lunch outside in the field, and I saw a big rattlesnake, walking across the area. I screamed, Marilou screamed, Dave took the shotgun and killed it. It was huge; we hang it on the tree's branch. Bob decided to make a belt out of it, so he skinned it, but the snake was too big, so it just hung on the wall in his bedroom, till it started smelling and we threw it away.

One day we received a call home from the Port Orange Sheriff. He said, "Sir, two teenagers are trying to break into your house, one of them says he is your son." We knew was Bob. He had forgotten the key and was trying to show the house to Les (his friend) and he was trying to prey open a window. Dave said to the officer, "Yes, he is my son, Bob, it is okay."

Bob has always been a kindhearted person. I had a Montego (my first car) and I kept telling everyone, "This is my casket when I die. I want to be buried in this car." One day Bob had just taken Marilou to school, I was at work and received a phone call "Madame, this is Officer Brown, your son has been in an accident". Without even thinking I said, "is my car okay, I am going to kill him." The Officer said, "Aren't you concerned about your son." I said, "Officer, I know he is fine, how about my car. I will be there in few minutes." I rushed to the scene; Bob was fine, my car destroyed. Two old ladies on the other side of the street, had a flat tire, and Bob had made a U-turn to go help them. A pickup truck hit him on the side. (I still think the pickup truck driver did it in purpose, he wanted a new truck). Anyway my car (my casket) was destroyed. Bob was all right, and I did not kill him. Bob would also drive with his knees, while eating a hamburger; there was a Burger King on the way to school.

Bob loved old cars so we bought him an old Chrysler. He worked on the car all the times. The problem was that since the car was old, Chrysler had stopped making parts for it, so he had to use different parts and be sure that they did fit. He had another car that he drove, till it ran out of oil, burned the engine up, and called us to pick him up. He worked for Disney World, and we still don't know how he hit a Disney bus. (Disney's busses are quite big, so easy to see).

We bought Bill a Porsche for $2,200. Nonna paid for half of it. He smashed it in few days. He was not familiar with the road, he took a corner too fast, and he hit an electrical pole. They also charged us for the pole $250 dollars. Bill was okay.

Bill also worked at Disney World, as a magician, he loved to be a magician, and he was quite good at it. That's where he met Sher, his first wife. (Sher worked at Lake Buena Vista). Bob also met Laura at Disney. Later Bill went to work for Sea World and designed the whole computer program on how to see all the shows and don't miss any rides. Bob also went to work for Sea World, and later on was delivering pizza. (He later joined the Army. Dave would have preferred the Air Force, since he was an Air Force man)

Philip Morris gave scholarship to children of employees. Bill got a scholarship, he was planning to go to MIT, but he married Sher and stayed home. Bob went to Valencia CC. Dave was teaching there. One day an English professor stopped Dave and said, "Where is your son, he never showed up for his final English exam". Bob had forgotten.

While Bill was at Bishop Moore in his 11th grade, he was allowed to take college courses. I was also taking courses; we both took statistics, a required course. Bill was busy with his High School so I did not mind helping him and pass him the answers for the final exam.

Bill and Bob were also in sports. They had a problem with their backs, so we took them to a specialist, who recommended taking gymnastic classes. So that summer I took all three to a gymnastic school.

Marilou enrolled in a drama class and she played a boy's part in "Little Mary Sunshine". She was really good.

Bishop Moore had a dress code; girls were not allowed to wear short skirts. All the girls, including Marilou used to roll up the skirts to the waist to make them shorter and then if they saw the principal they would pull the skirt back down.

Marilou had a bad habit, when she got mad, she would lock herself in the room. Dave and I did not like that, so we took the lock out of her bedroom's door. Finally she saw how dangerous it was.

I passed room inspection once a week. The boy's rooms were okay, Marilou's room a mess. Drawers open, clothes hanging from the drawers. I finally talked with Dave about it and said, "I quit, I will not check her room, and she can keep her room closed, so I will not see that mess." Finally Marilou saw that I had given up inspection to her room, and she started cleaning. It had worked. Now as an adult she keeps a spotless house. Teenagers!. What can I say!

While working for Southern Gold, I had became a Customs Drawback specialist (drawback, meant, we imported orange concentrate from foreign countries, Mexico, Brazil, even Israel, then we exported to foreign countries, especially Europe. We had to pay duty when we imported but we could collect back $.34 cents for the duty when we exported, as long as modifications had been done to the product). I loved my job, I had to take frequent trips to Miami, and I took Bill with me. I did not know that later on this knowledge would allow me many benefits.

Then we had a bad freeze. Philip Morris dumped both 7up and our company. I received one year of severance pay and 5 stocks. We opened a Video Store 'Cosmic Video'; I worked many hours, 6 days a week. Dave would come after school and help me out while I drove Marilou to her ballet's classes. The business lasted for about a year and then we had to close it down when Movie Gallery moved next door.

I had been going to college, first Valencia (they gave me one year college from my Italian studies), and then to Rollins College, (I worked in the daytime and went to school in the evening. In the summer I would take accelerated courses, going every night for two weeks.) I had received a Bachelor's degree in Social Studies and a Master's degree in education, so I went subbing with the hope to receive a teaching job. I got a job for three months as a sub at Robinswood Junior High. I was teaching geography. One day, while we were watching a video, someone in the class said, "Mrs. Wills, he has done it again; he is peeing on the floor". There was a student doing exactly that. I lasted 3 months, after that, I subbed for Bishop Moore, and for Dave at Evans High school when he went for varicose veins operation. Then I landed a job at West Orange High School. I stayed a year. I had 40 students in my Spanish class, till they moved some out. The school had many rednecks and they were fighting all the times. One of the gang leaders was in my Spanish class, and he had taken a liking to me. He thought I was a great teacher. He used to tell me, "Mrs. Wills, I will never use this, but you have helped me a lot. Thanks for having faith in me". At the end of the school year they decided to riot. The young man came to me and said, "Sit here, Mrs. Wills, don't worry, no one will hurt you or your car"(I had just recently purchased my all favorite car, a Lincoln Town Car). While all the other teachers were running around in panic, I quietly did what the young man had told me, and I felt very safe. Teachers were coming by me and saying, "Why are you so calm, there is a riot going on". I just smiled.

In 1980 I felt a lump in my right breast. I told Dave, I started crying, and the thought of dying and leave Dave and my children was unbearable. We prayed and I did not even tell my mother. I went to see Dr. Curry, they ran some tests, and I had many cysts in my right breast, but was not cancerous. So every year I have to take a mammogram and a sonogram. (Later when we went to Germany, while teaching for Dodds, the hospital wanted my original X-rays to compare them. I had the X-rays with me, but I refused to leave them at the hospital. It was a good thing, because when we left in 1996, they had lost all my X-rays, but I still had my original ones.) Last time, they found a black spot, they were thinking about a biopsy. When I went back, the spot had gone away. Dave was a big support; he came with me every time I had to go for a mammogram. Everyone liked him at Dr. Curry's office.

Marilou had become a beautiful dancer, and she wanted to dance in Europe. She felt it would have been hard to get a dancing job in New York and she loved Europe. So Dave and I applied to work as teachers for the Department of Defense. We filled out our applications and send it to Washington. In the meantime we took another trip to Europe for 22 days. This time my mother did not come with us. We went to Bonn. Marilou took some classes there; she had made up a song, saying Bonn. Bonn . . . Bonn . . . . and sang all the way to Italy. She was able to take some classes in Florence. She thought she was fat, so at every airport or for what matters every scales she saw, she would weigh herself.

In Europe there were scales everywhere, and faithfully Marilou would weigh herself. Of course she had to change Kilograms into pounds. Also she was always very nervous before a performance. We always left 2 hours before she had to perform. Dave would be driving; he was a careful driver. Marilou would say, "Papa, I'm going to be late, drive faster," and Dave would say, "We'll get there when we get there." This of course infuriated Marilou. Then when we finally arrived, he would say, "See, we are not late, you have plenty time," and he was right.

We had decided to sell our home in Pine Hills, we rented it to a couple, and we had requested no pets. Later on we found out that they had been 6 dogs in the house. We lost $10,000 from the sale.

While waiting for the job in Europe to open (we had requested Italy), we found a teaching job in Lumberton, North Carolina, Dave at a High School; I at two elementary schools. I was teaching French as a second language in two different schools, from K thru 2nd grade.

We rented an apartment. Every time we said the word Lumberton, a zit would come out on Marilou's face. The apartment was not very nice.

A giant must have lived there before, because all the cabinets were at least 6 feet tall, I could barely see myself in the mirror, and the shower would always flood. I was teaching at two schools, one for the rich and one for the poor. I used to take supplies from the rich school and bring it to the poor (mostly Indians from the forgotten tribe). While I was teaching French, I had said to my students: "if you give me chicken pox, I will 'coupe' la tête' (cut your head off). I never had chicken pox, both Bill and Bob had it, but neither Marilou nor I ever caught it. One day, a student was absent, and I received a phone call from a parent. She said, "Mrs. Wills, would you please talk to Angela. She was out with chicken pox, she is afraid to come back to school because you said you would cut her head off. I tried to explain to her that you were joking and she does not believe me." I talked to Angela and told her so. The child came back, but she stayed all the way in the back of the class, watching me. I had forgotten that at that age, they would believe me. They learned well, they even learned la Marseillaise (French national anthem), which they performed at the end of the school year.

Lumberton had a very strange custom. At Christmas time we would have decorations and luminaries, a truck loaded with poor people, mainly Indians, were brought thru our neighborhood to see the lights. That must have been very sad for these people that they could not afford it.

In the meantime we kept asking Washington about our papers. They had lost all our applications, but they did have an opening in Wuerzburg, a math and reading job. I took it. Dave came and taught also but not thru Dodds. When the principal asked me, "Why can't you stay in Lumberton", as politely as I could, I said, "I really prefer to go to Europe, sorry".

We stored many things in our Port Orange house, and left the dog behind (he later died, bitten by a snake).

We used to take frequent trips to Florida to check on our homes and we used to stop at Dennis restaurant. One time we stopped at Dennis in Georgia (Dave loved Dennis' breakfast), at the next table we noticed that the couple had called the waiter and had left. They had found a roach on the table. From then on Marilou refused to eat at Dennis and so did I. A year ago from the hospital, Dave and I stopped at the Dennis. Dave had breakfast; I had a cup of coffee.

# Wurzburg

My job was at Wurzburg, a brand new school. There weren't openings at my school for Dave and he ended up teaching at Bamberg, about one hour away from our house to six graders. Later on he moved to my school, but Dr. Kroon and Dave did not get along very well (she was not well liked), and he was not re-employed. So he went teaching for the City College of Chicago. He had fun teaching for college students (military personnel), and I also taught there in the evening Pre-Algebra. Marilou took one of my classes.

She had been dancing at Nurenberg. One day she was practicing a jump, and fell the wrong way, hurt her hip and she stopped dancing but went to college (University of Maryland) for a Business degree. While she danced in Nurenberg, she performed in many places. One day they were performing in one of the hall room in the Gasthouse, and suddenly a bunch of men dressed in tutu came out and started doing ballet. It was very funny, and definitely unusual. Dave and I laughed all thru the performance; it was a parody of Swan Lake.

I loved teaching in Wurzburg, I taught French and Math. We lived in Iphofen, about 40 miles from Wurzburg. We took many walks thru the woods. Marilou, Dave and I used to walk by this cornfield, and since Dave loved corn, we thought to pick up some corn when it was ready. So we did, wondering why the Germans where not picking up all this corn. We cooked it, water was pinkish and it tested funny. We threw it away, later we asked our landlord about the corn, and he told us that the corn was being grown for the sole purpose to feed the pigs. Yuck. We also went strawberry picking. Marilou and I were picking strawberry, but eating the big ones, till the lady said, "You are paying by the weight; please do not eat while you pick them". We were quite embarrassed, and we stopped.

Teachers were great; Marilou subbed for me many times, and was paid pretty well. Dave's health was getting worse, and he made many trips to the hospital with pneumonia.

The hardest time was during Desert Storm. Most of our military personnel had gone to Iraq, leaving their families behind. The children were extremely distressed, we did send cards to all the parents, but children had hard time to cope with the war. We also had many threats at the base. For a month every time I would be going to school, a MP will be outside; there had been a bomb threat. They would check the whole building, while the students and the teachers would walk to the Theater on the base and wait for the okay. We had to walk thru the landing field of the Black Hawk helicopters. It went on for a month; it was during the winter time and quite cold. Finally they caught the person that was making these phone calls. He was a High School student, mother German and father American GI. They were shipped back to the States.

We had a station wagon (the famous one that overheated) and we decided to sell it and replace it with the Lumina. A German guy offered us 2000 deutschmarks. We accepted, he gave us a deposit of 500 DM and told us he will be back in two weeks to pick the car up and pay the balance. We waited, waited, time came by, and he never showed up, we did not have his name; he had paid us cash. Finally after two months we re-sold the car. Who knows what had happened to the guy. We had made a pretty good profit on a lemon car.

I wanted for Marilou to make some friends, I felt bad that she was spending so much time with us, but she would always say, "I enjoy spending time with both of you, stop feeling bad."

We went to the Eagle's nest, Hitler's summer residence. We went in the salt mine, and walked all the way up to the nest. When we returned home, I was very sick. The doctor put me in the hospital, I had lost 3 pints of blood, and she wondered how I had not had a heart attack while climbing to the nest. I was in the hospital during the 4th of July and Dave and Marilou went to see the fireworks on the base. They were giving me IV but I had lost so much blood, that they could not find my veins. They kept punching holes in both my arms; finally a Colonel came by and told them to put morphine on the holes so I would not be in so much pain. I had to go back to the U.S. for an operation. Marilou was supposed to join us later on (she was in the last week of her college class), but when she went to the airport and boarded the plane there was a breach of security. She was scared and she did not want to fly especially by herself. She cried on the phone and I told her not to worry. I was doing fine at Port Orange. Before the operation we stayed at Bill and Lisa's apartment. They had planned a trip, so they told us we could use their house, and we would be closer to the hospital, in Winter Park.

When Marilou and Michael (at that time her boyfriend) came to pick us up at the airport, Marilou drove our BMW (we had been told by the seller that these BMW were build to meet American standards, and so you could not drive them faster than 127 miles per hour, the gas would stop pumping and the car will slow down). Marilou, when she picked us up said, "You know it is true the car does slow down when you go faster than 127mph." We were horrified that she would drive that fast. Her answer was, "there was no traffic on the autobahn".

We took frequent trips to Austria. One day while driving back to Germany, Dave was driving, Marilou was in the back seat, and kept complaining that he was going too slowly, and he should go faster. Poor Dave was getting very nervous. Finally he sped up, and soon a polizei car appeared from behind, flashing lights. Dave stopped, said he did not speak German, the policeman in perfect English said, "Sir, we have no speed limits on the autobahn, but when we do, you have to obey them". Dave apologized and the policeman did not give him a ticket. Marilou was quiet for the rest of the trip back home.

Marilou loved to drive fast, and she received many warning. We used to pick on her by saying the German police headquarters must have a file on her and say, "Oh, there is Marilou again". One time a policeman on the motorcycle stopped her, and she talked him out of the ticket. Unfortunately any time she was stopped by a policeman, they would call my principal at the school, since she was my dependent. One time, they called Dave and said, "We have a picture of a young woman, driving and not stopping at the stop sign". Dave said, "Oh, that's my daughter, let me give you her name, and where to reach her ". Marilou got very angry, but you could tell from the photo, that was a young woman driving and not me, besides I was at school teaching.

We also went to Denmark, Copenhagen and saw the little mermaid. (I just saw the video that Marilou took in 1993 for the trip, and also when Bill came to Paris at Christmas time, and the Verdun battlefield)

We took many school field trips. Many of the students and teachers favorite was the Sinsheim's museum. On one occasion, a captain's daughter decided to steal some items from the vendors. She was caught, the German police came, the American police came, it was a mess and quite embarrassing.

We also went to the Nurenberg's zoo. One time, we were caught in what in Germany is called a stau (traffic jam). We could not call parents, and at that time there were no cell phone. We did not arrive till late in the night, most parents had gone home, and teachers ended up driving students at home.

Our principal was not very well liked. One day, it was snowing horribly; I drove very slowly to the school. A school bus came by going in the opposite directions, my students hanging from the window saying, "Hi, Mrs. Wills". I was wondering, what is going on, I am going to the school and they are leaving. No one had called the teachers to tell them to stay home; she had endangered the life of all the teachers. She used to stand by the door to be sure that no one was late. She even reprimanded her assistant principal, Ms. Laffoley, for being late one morning. We used to have fire drills, and she had established a series of rules. We all had to go outside, and we could only come back inside after the drill was over and by rows. One day, during a fire drill, it was snowing; we went outside. The children were not wearing any coats. When I was cleared, I just took my students in without respecting the row call. She came upstairs, called me outside and said, "Mrs. Wills, you have broken ranks by going inside before the other teachers." My answer to her, "I had many sick students, I was not about to stay outside and have them get worse." She did not like my answer, but my duty was first to the students and not to her.

One day we had a bomb threat, the assistant principal was there, he called the MP, he sent all the students out of the building, but kept the teachers inside and asked us to look behind file cabinets for bombs. Unbelievable. He got reprimanded for endangering our lives.

On weekend we also took many Volksmarches, either 10 kilometers or 20. Price was a beer mug, and we have plenty of these. Dave was doing well, except later it was hard for him to complete the march.

We were allowed to travel for free back to the States once a year. In 1994 we went to Frankfurt Air Terminal, we had just checked in our luggage. I noticed that around the plane, that we were supposed to take, there were armed German Police with German shepherds dogs. We were called in, one by one, to stand by the plane and next to our luggage. Apparently, a suitcase had gone thru and they did not know whom it belonged to. We finally boarded the plan. The pilot said not very reassuring words, "I THINK we are OK". When we arrived in New York, everyone clapped with a sign of relief.

While in Germany I had received a call from a lawyer, Don Beach. Philip Morris needed a drawback specialist to review some of the Southern Gold drawbacks. So in June Marilou and I left for New York, Dave stayed behind. We received the royal treatment. I was paid pretty well, but it was a lot of work. I met Stew Bakula, and later he told us that he was the father of Scott Bakula, who was in the show "Quantum Leap". While I was working in the warehouse, Marilou would stay in the hotel, with room service and watching many times the then popular movie "Dancing with the Wolves". We also went downtown sightseeing. We even took the subway. Later they rented us a car. One day we went to the garage, entered a car, and couldn't figure out why the key did not work, and then we realized that we had entered the wrong car. We laughed our heart out. Quickly we got out, and find our car. We also went to the Empire State Building and took a picture with a fake King Kong at the top. I worked for them till 1996. In 1996, I went back to New York for the last time, we had just returned from Germany. Dave this time came with me, and while in New York we went to see "Cats", but we had to leave New York because Dave was not breathing well.

As part of our curriculum we had to take many outside courses. One was in Munich and dealt with German culture and past history.

In January of 1995 I went for a workshop to Nurenberg. My friend Julia came with me. Dave and her husband also named Dave were supposed to drive along with us, but instead they decided to stay home. I drove my BMW; it was icy and snowing. I was driving 20 mph; the car hit what is called "black ice" and started to slide. It took a quick moment to decide if I should either hit the truck in front of me, or the tree. I chose the tree, good decision. The truck driver stopped and gave us assistance; in fact he stayed with me until the ambulance arrived. The fireman had to break the windshield and the side door to get me out; I was pinned inside. My first thought was: "My car insurance is going to go up", but it did not because it was not my fault. They notified the principal. The principal notified Marilou (she was subbing). Marilou cried at the news. Then I think either Marilou or the principal notified Dave. Marilou told me later that when Dave drove by the car, and saw the condition of the car, he started crying. He thought he had lost me. I was lucky. I only broke 8 ribs, a gash in my leg and bruised my spleen. Food was great, there was an Italian doctor on the staff, and I received very good care. They kept giving me a shot in the stomach every day for thrombosis. I finally asked when they could stop giving me that painful shot. The nurse said, "As soon as you start walking". The next day, I was out of the bed and walking up and down the corridor of the hospital. I left the Nurenberg hospital after 45 days. Dave, Marilou and Michael (now her husband) came to visit me all the times. I had to go back to the States because of my wrists, also damaged during the crash. With Dave continuing health problems, and with Marilou now married to Michael and with a child, I decided that was the time to go back to the States and leave Dodds. We had previously returned to Florida to buy land. We looked everywhere, we did not want 2 acres again like at Port Orange. We finally purchased one acre in Rivercrest. I had bought a magazine with different house plans. Marilou, Dave and I chose the one that we had later built.

A big house, so also Marilou, Michael and the baby had a place to stay. Dave, Marilou and Alessandra left first; I stayed behind for 45 lonely days, (I cried every night). I had a fear of driving in the snow, afraid that the car will slide again, so we moved from Iphofen to a city near my school. (We had lived in Iphofen for 5 years. Iphofen was a very old city with roman walls still standing. It had a pond that will freeze during winter and the whole city including Dave and Marilou went to skate. They bought ice skates; I would just hold Marilou as she skated along. Dave had been a good roller skater when he was young.) Still, I was a nervous wreck, as soon as it started snowing, I'll shake, even now when it rains too hard, my heart starts beating really fast. I was very lonely; I counted every day till I could fly to the U.S. and be with my family. At Christmas I left, they operated on my wrists and in March, I went back to Germany with Dave to finish my tour. We begged John, our builder, to finish our house so Marilou did not have to drive from Port Orange to her job at AAA in Lake Mary. He kept his word, and Marilou and Alessandra were able to move in our new home. Furniture had arrived, so I felt good about going back to Germany. Michael was in Alabama to finish his tour of duty. While at Port Orange, I received the news that my friend Julia had died in Germany. I was very sad for many days.

Marilou and Alessandra stayed at my new home. It was tough for Marilou and she did her best in keeping everything together. When I was in Florida, I went to see Dr. White, my hand specialist, Dave and Alessandra came with me every time and everyone admired that little girl, then before we will leave to go back to Port Orange, we would stop at the restaurant across the street, and all the employees would come and talk with Alessandra.

While in Germany, Dave took care of Alessandra when her mom was subbing. When Alessandra was about 6 months old, Dave had placed her on the bed; she wasn't crawling yet. He walked away for just a second and heard a noise, Alessandra had fallen off the bed, and she was now crawling. Dave called Marilou, took her to the hospital, she was fine, but the military were giving Marilou and Michael a very hard time.

Next to Iphofen, there was a little town Kitzingen (that's where Marilou and Michael married). In Kitzingen there was an old cemetery. We went to visit it. We saw a casket surrounded by big gates. Each gate had bats welded in. We asked the locales, who was buried there. They told us it was Dracula's grave. True or not, it was quite impressive and interesting.

## Back to the States

We came back to the States to join Marilou and Alessandra; Michael was still finishing his last few months in Alabama. I found a job downtown. I had mailed over 300 applications; I even applied to teach at a Muslim School. Marilou suggested that I apply to AAA also. I really wanted to go back to teaching, so I could spend the summer with Dave.

I found a job with Florida Business; I loved the job. I dealt with Germany, South America, and Europe. Still I kept checking with schools. When a job opened at Tuskawilla Middle School, I called to set up an interview. When the secretary answered I said, "I am calling for an interview, you don't need to interview anyone else. I am the right person for the job." The secretary told me later that the principal had liked very much my spunkiness. I was offered the job at Tuskawilla Middle School. I was very happy, since Dave's health was declining. I could be off in the summer; I would be working only 196 days a year. I always loved accounting, but teaching math would still place me in what I liked, and Dave was much too important to me.

When I told my supervisor that I was leaving on Monday, he offered me more money, but I refused. I felt bad by leaving with only one day notice, so that weekend I went downtown and worked for free, updating all the files. Dave used to drive me downtown, because parking was so hard and he also did not like for me to go in the parking garage by myself.

He was very protective and an old gentleman, too many crimes, so he would drive me in the morning and pick me up in the evening every single day.

I stayed at Tuskawilla Middle School for over 4 years; it was 45 minutes drive one way. Finally I moved to Rock Lake, much closer to home, and to Dave.

Alessandra was a joy, we had a pool installed, and she was so cute in the pool. We wanted to be sure that Alessandra would be swimming, so first I took her to YMCA. The young instructor, would take a bunch of kids, put a winglet on their arms, and make them do movements, by singing, "The wheels on the bus go round, round . . ." After two weeks and listening to the same song over and over, I did not see any improvement, so I asked the teacher when she would actually teach her how to swim. She said, "I do give private lessons". I took her away from YMCA and went to a swimming place on W.F. Williams. The teacher, Ms. Allison, was tough. She threw Alessandra in the pool, and she said, "swim". It broke my heart. I tried not to look. Dave came once, and could not stand it. But she learned how to swim; it was worth it.

Since I had many Armani and Swaroski in my living room, I used to call the room "the forbidden zone". Alessandra knew to stay away from it and even when her friends would come and visit, she would say, "stay away from the forbidden zone."

When we took Alessandra to Disney, she loved the characters, but was afraid of them. Dave would stay in long lines so that they would autograph her book. One time we went in a Disney restaurant 'The Crystal Palace', we did not know they were characters walking around. We sat at the table after waiting quite a long time, and a character walked in. Alessandra saw him, screamed, and rushed out the door. I chased her down, while Dave was gathering my purse. We left and went to eat at Pinocchio.

My mother had left in 1992 to stay with Bob and Laura. (They were stationed in Germany. That is where Alyssa was born). In 1996 she moved back with us. It was getting hard between taking care of my mother and Dave, so with a heavy heart (I regret till now), I placed my mother in an assisted living facility. First I tried to see if she could go to Italy with my brother, but my brother health wasn't good either. My mother health became worse, she fell, we took her to the hospital, and they had to place a tube in her stomach so she could eat. She kept pulling the tube out. She did not remember my name; she kept calling me Mimmo. I moved her to another place. Every day I went to visit her with Dave, and every day I would cry on the way home. Dave and I felt bad. He knew I was hurting. We went one time and she was laying in filth, I complained to the administration, but I could see that nothing would have been done. We had decided to either find a better facility or move her back with us with a nurse and build an annexation to our house. But by the time the arrangements were about to be made, she had died on July 3, 2000. I was at McDonald with Alessandra and Dave. Marilou called me to give me the news. I felt so guilty, and will feel that way till I die. I should have done more, but with Dave's health getting worse, I was at a breaking point.

Dave's health was declining, he was operated for prostate cancer with seedlings, and his COPD was getting worse. Only 40% of his lungs were functioning. Michael finished his military duty and moved with us. A year later Marilou and Michael moved in their own apartment and later in their first house. Dave would go pick Alessandra up from school. (This was for the 5 years that she was in elementary school). Many times he would sit in the car for over an hour, to be sure that he was the first one in line. Everyone would talk to him, and he would bring candies to the children when they left school. (Funny one: Michael went to Woodland to pick Alessandra up one day and they kept asking him, "Who are you," "I'm her father", "Yes, but we see her grandfather picking her up every day"). When I moved from Tuskawilla Middle to Rock Lake I would take Alessandra to school and Dave would pick her up. Later when she went to my school, I will pick her up and take her home; Dave would pick her up on Wednesday to take her to golf. I think Dave missed these years when Alessandra was in elementary school. He scheduled his doctor's appointment not to interfere in picking her up.

Alessandra became interested in golf, so after school Dave would take her to golf, and sit in the car for a couple of hours, till either Michael or Marilou would come. He was many times upset because he couldn't go and see her play in tournaments. He kept telling me, "I take her every day to golf, why can't I see her playing in tournaments". Marilou had rightly told me, that in many competitions they did not allow a golf cart, and Dave couldn't walk the 18 holes. I would explain it to Dave, but he was still upset. He adored Alessandra, kept calling her Marilou many times. When Alessandra did not golf, they went home and Dave taught her how to play cribbage, but she could not beat him. Alessandra was very jealous when Dave would compliment another little girl. He loved children, but when he realized that this hurt Alessandra, he was very careful not to compliment or talk with other children when Alessandra was with him, so he would not hurt her feelings. We did not know Sharayah and Alyssa very well, since Bob was in the military. They did come and visit us, and we knew a little more about them. Bob and Laura also kept us posted with photos and what they were accomplishing. Alyssa has a beautiful voice and they send us videos of some of her performances. She plans to work at Disney World as a princess and a performer and go to college. Sharayah wants to be in police field (like the CSI program), and lately I heard she might join the Air Force. (Dave would have been happy). When Bill was married with Sher, they had a daughter Patti. When Bill, Sher and Patti came to Germany to visit us, we went to Italy all together and spent a wonderful time. Patti was really cute (I am sure she still is) and Dave and her got along very well. Bill got divorced and later married Lisa, Nicole was born (Dave and I have never met Nicole. I am sure she is also very cute). After the divorce Bill came to visit us again in Germany. At Christmas time we took him to Disney World in France, and he was making fun of 'Café au lait' by saying 'Café ole'.

For the first time only girls were being born in the Wills' family. Marilou's birth must have broken the spell.

Dave's health was getting worse, and I was really worried. Many times during the night I would wake up and check if he was breathing. Dave had heart problems and so he had open-heart surgery and a valve put in. I was really scared that he would leave me. We made many trips to the hospital and I spent many nights sleeping in a chair next to his bed. It was very hard for both of us but he did come home. He still had breathing problems. I asked the doctor if I could give him one of my lungs, and also Bill offered, but the doctor said that a new lung would not have helped him with his COPD.

We did take two cruises with Marilou, Michael and Alessandra, and certainly enjoyed it. We wanted to travel more, but Dave's health was getting worse especially his breathing.

Dave and I used to joke around saying that we should have had 4 children, so we could spend 3 months with each of them, free of expenses. I used to pick on Marilou by saying that between ballet shoes and costumes and so on she owned me $350,000 and I wanted it all in cash at one time. I don't know how I came up with that figure but Dave and I had a good laugh.

## Meeting with President Bush

Dave's health was not improving. He had decided to go to Texas to see his son, David, from his previous marriage. We flew to Austin and rented a car and visited his son and his large family. His son's wife was dying of cancer. Dave had a good time. We went to the courthouse in Austin. While standing outside, a motorcade stopped and a man jumped from it and approached us (surrounded by many security men). He shook our hand and said, "I'm governor Bush, where are you folks from." We told him from Florida. His brother, Jeb Bush, was at that time governor of Florida. Since Jeb Bush was running again for governor, we suggested that he tell his brother to choose a woman as his running mate. He said that he would certainly tell him and he welcomed us to Texas.

He left. If we had just known that he would someday be president, we could have taken a picture with him, and ask him for an autograph. But it certainly was nice to know that we had actually met the future President of the United States.

## Our last trip to Europe

Trip June 3, thru June 22, 1999. June 3 we left from Orlando to Boston. We stayed in Boston for 5 hours, and then we took Swiss Air to Zurich, Switzerland. We had rented a car at the airport, from Budget Car rental. The car we wanted was not available, the clerk tried to call around but to not avail. We wanted a car with a trunk instead of a station wagon, anyway we took the car, the clerk only handed us the keys and we looked for the car on our own. We found the car, I drove, could not find the lights so we asked a passer by. He showed us, we left the airport and suddenly an "air bag" light showed up on the board. Since we were not very familiar with the Citroen car, we stopped at a station. The attendant said that perhaps we needed to take the car back because of the Air bag light. We turned around, went back to the airport; Dave went back to the 'Budget Rent a Car' clerk. As he told me later, the clerk had left and a lady clerk was there and said it was quite normal for the car to have a flashing light saying "Air Bag". Dave came back, told me this, we tried to get out of the airport but could not, and the ticket did not work. I parked in a reserved parking space; Dave went back to the desk clerk and she said we needed to pay the fee. Dave said he wouldn't since we had returned for a defective car, finally the lady signed something on the card, we were lucky, a policeman was there and he let us out. (Remark-Swiss Air is a good airline; food and wine were excellent, except we couldn't watch movies because our screen was too small, and I couldn't get comfortable enough to sleep.) Anyway we went toward Austria. We found a 4 stars hotel. Mountains were still covered with snow. Alps were grand.

We went downtown, purchased Italian crosswords puzzle books, a cow for Alessandra, a T-shirt for Dave and Michael, a table linen for

Marilou and I. Next day, we went to the Swarovski factory, the place had changed, it was now in a mountain with Janus eyes sparkling protecting the crystals. They gave us free entrance tickets, because I was a member in the US. Dave got tired, sat in the snack bar for members only; I looked around and purchased some beautiful pieces for Alessandra, Marilou and myself, plus I decided to have another salamander pin and the gentleman kindly made one for me. The girl who talked with us, was Austrian, planned to become a music teacher, her mother was a biologist, chemist, and teacher. We discussed school system and how students had changed over the years. Finally we left; we were supposed to go to Verona/Vicenza at Hotel Bologna. The Alps were gorgeous, weather beautiful, driving pleasant. I did all the driving; Dave was pretty tired and kept falling asleep in the car. But I was happy he was next to me. We went to hotel Bologna, unfortunately the manager of the hotel had changed and we had not called in advance. Anyway we had decided to stay 3 days; we went to eat at the "Due Colonne", a pizzeria that we had used as eatery before. The new owner told us that the old owner's husband had died, and she was trying to make the best of it. Dave had the usual, spaghetti and meatballs or as he called "Spaghetti Bolognese"; I had chicken. She offered us an aperitif (Lemoncello). We went back to the hotel to sleep, watched Italian TV. The next day we drove to Venice. Then we parked, took the Vaporetto.

As I had done many times before, I argued about the high prices of parking the car. Venice was being cleaned and restored with money from all over the world. Venice is always spectacular. We went into the tower elevator, took beautiful pictures, then the Chiesa of San Marco. I went upstairs and took pictures of the real horses (made out of gold taken from Costantinopoli), outside there are the fake one. Took pictures of the Ponte dei Sospiri, walked towards Ponte Rialto, purchased some beautiful Murano glass, purchased Dave a hat with Venice logo, and for Alessandra a cute umbrella. Then we sat at a coffee shop; Dave had a beer for $20.00 while I was walking, and looking for glass (all too expensive). It was late afternoon so we took the Vaporetto back and drove to Hotel Bologna.

We had supper at the 2 Colonne. The next day we went to Vicenza to the NATO base, purchased some more crystal, and find out that we could mail packages to our self in the U.S. as long as they weighted 1 pound. We decided to go to Camp Darby (Pisa) and try. We went back to the hotel (after washing clothes) and went to Verona. We took pictures of the Arena, tried to go to an old restaurant. We had been there before and couldn't find it. I purchased some more crosswords puzzle books. Went back and decided to eat at the Soave restaurant in Soave, but it was closed, so we went to the 2 Colonne and had pizza. When we returned to our room, we found a plate of fresh fruit; the owner of the hotel was apologizing for not having given us a better room. We left Pisa and arrived at Camp Darby, mailed our self our packages. The billeting was not very nice but cheap.

We decided to go downtown Pisa and took some pictures of the tower of Pisa. We drove around for 1 and half-hour, all roads were one way. I asked many people how to get to the tower. Finally I stopped a car of Carabinieri, and they told me to follow them, we did and they brought us directly to the tower. Again we had to ask and this man said, "You know you are the fourth person asking the same thing." Finally we found the tower, still leaning, took pictures and decided to eat there, we had some good food, Cappuccino and left. The next day we drove to Firenze and I guess the gods were looking upon us, because for the first time in more than 30 times that we had gone to Florence I drove directly to the Hotel. I did go thru a street that it was intended for busses only. We parked right in front, unloaded. The manager remembered us, gave us a nice room. I parked in the garage down 2 doors, that afternoon we walked to Ponte Vecchio, looked at the beautiful gold displayed, took some beautiful pictures of the sunset and purchased a gold necklace for Michael. We decided to eat at Bibo. The manager and the cook had changed. Food was not that good and Dave found a shrimp shell in his famous spaghetti Bolognesi. We told them, he apologized and offered us a drink. We decided never to go back there. Back to the hotel, next day we went to see the David, to the "Belle Arti" Museum, purchased some souvenirs and walked around. The last day we went to Palazzo Pitti museum, shopped again for clothes, toys, and shoes (went to the Mercato for wallets and shoes). We also found the shoe place that we had used before and Dave bought some shoes. I called Rosetta and told her I will be in Salerno soon. The next day we left for Salerno arrived there, called Rosetta, she told me how to get to her house. Franco helped us park the car. Rosetta had changed. We went upstairs and I was talking, and she informed me that the use of my Italian verbs were incorrect. I said, "I don't think so". She said, "As a professor you should be doing much better." The bed was uncomfortable, we had nowhere to bathe. Rosetta was loud and used profanity, and sexual references that made me uncomfortable. Next day we went to Naples, took pictures of where I went to school. We had a pizza. We took the whole family to a restaurant of their choice. It was extremely expensive, I felt cheated. Too bad my friend had changed so much; maybe I had changed. We left, went back to Camp Darby, and then we decided to go to Massa Carrara. We drove, up the mountains, very interesting. We looked at Romans and pre-Romans objects. We drove up to the Cave and purchased some statues. They were pretty heavy. Returned to Camp Darby and mailed packages again. We stayed in Aosta for two days, went thru the Grand San Bernard. We took a side trip to Lourdes and I got some holy water that I carried all the way up a hill, I prayed very hard for Dave to get better. We left from Genève, and back to New York and Orlando. We purchased many souvenirs, but all the remembrance was in our hearts and our brains. I miss Europe but I also miss my family. I hoped we could go back. I did not know that was the last time that Dave and I will go to Europe. I did all the driving, the moving of the suitcases, I was tired but happy. Dave's health was getting worse. Dave had talked about after I retired to spend a couple of months in Italy.

Dave and I were totally dedicated to our family, and we tried to give our children all the things that we never had. When they were growing up we took the children and my mother all over the United States. When in Germany, we took Marilou with us on all the trips all over Europe. We went to Denmark on a boat; I just saw a video that Marilou had taken of our cabin, which was extremely small. Then later when she married Michael, they both joined us on all the trips, like St. Michelle (gorgeous), Paris, Italy. When we came back to the States we went all together to Las Vegas to visit Michael's mother, his stepfather. They were enjoyable times. As all good Italian family, we all feel that family comes first.

## Last 5 years

Dave used to prepare my lunch and put candies in my lunch bag, every day when I went to work. He would fix the collar of my shirt, check if I was wearing make up, lipstick, straightened my hair in the back, opened the garage door for me and waved goodbye with a kiss. During the night when I would get up and go to the bathroom, he would wake up and always ask, "Are you okay?" I would answer, "Yes, don't worry", and I said the same thing to him. When I left for school I called him as soon as I got there, called him again at lunch and during plan to make sure he was taking his medication, and call him when I left from school. I miss these phone calls. On our 40th anniversary cruise, we did not tell Marilou and Michael that while on a side trip on our cruise, he had fallen very hard on the stones (we just told them that he hurt himself on some branches). I was astonished on how the other people reacted, by running to his aid; except for the bus driver, he did not do anything. I was quite irked. We had fun, he thought it was great that the waiter would cut his food, and be so nice to him. It was a wonderful anniversary; I was hoping to go again for our 45th anniversary. It was hard on me. I had to carry the entire luggage to the car till finally someone helped us loading in the trunk. But no matter what, even if I was tired, I loved it.

I did everything at the house but Dave was next to me. He hated to see me working so hard, but I didn't care. Now that he is not here I realize that he was my strength. He was the one giving me the strength and the will to work. My strength and my will are slowly slipping away. I took care of Dave, my soul late, my husband, my best friend, my life, the father I never had. He had told me, "Rose, when the next time I go to the hospital, I'll not leave the hospital alive." These words haunted me, and I tried so hard to keep him out of the hospital. I would not be talking about his 35 days at the hospital, about his sickness, the guilt I have been feeling for not spending more time with him at the hospital. I think I should have not listened to Dr. Guerrero and have him stop taking the amiodorome, maybe not go to the restaurant where he fell. I should not have gone to the movies with Marilou and Michael but staying by his side day and night. Every night and every morning I greet Dave's picture with a hello and that I love him and hope to soon join him. I miss watching TV with him. We held hands and sometimes he would doze off, and other times I would, but we were always holding hands and sit closely. Now while I watch TV, I look at his picture on the wall, and talk to him. I have hard times going to church, because I remember both of us sitting next to each other, holding hands, he whispering in my hear: "What is the priest saying", because he had forgotten to wear his earring aid. I would tell him and during the sign of peace, we would give each other a kiss, and we will tell each other, "I love you." Now there is no one except his spirit. During the day, I would call to be sure he was okay. Many times he would forget to hang up the phone, so I would get a busy signal, so I would first call Marilou, then my neighbor Jo, and if she was not there, I would call Brenda, to check on him, to be sure he was okay. I miss him especially in the evening, when I am all by myself. In the daytime, I keep myself busy, especially at school, with Alessandra and my friends. It is in the night when I am left alone with my memories. He had told me that if I died first, he would stop taking his medications, because he could not live without me, and I told him I felt the same way about him.

I would translate for Dave jokes from my Italian crosswords puzzle book, and he will laugh away. Every night we watched his favorite show "Jeopardy". He was so happy when he knew the answers. Sometimes I would also and we laughed about, saying to each other how smart we were. Even when he was in the hospital, I will call him and we would share the answers by phone, or I will stay at the hospital with him and watch Jeopardy together. It was his favorite show. Now I still watch the show. It is a tradition, and I ask him if he agrees with my answers. (No, I am not crazy). I used to joke and call him a barbarian; because of the way he would eat his orange, by cutting it in half. He would laugh. By Roman's standards I would also be considered a barbarian, because I was not a Roman citizen.

I was at the school, during planning, when the hospital called me. Eden, another math teacher, drove me to the hospital. I knew he was dying, even if I refused to accept it. I spent the 15th of August next to him. Marilou and Michael had told me to go home. I told them I wanted to stay by his side. I did not want him to feel alone. They left; I stayed by his side, not sleeping, just caressing his hand and kissing him. I watched his monitors, hoping for a miracle.

The next morning, August 16, Dave died, the only thing that I could say was, "Who am I'm going to watch Jeopardy with". Obviously I did not know what I was saying. (I had called Marilou; Bob, Laura and Alyssa where on the way from Arizona.) Michael was standing by me, he placed a hand on my shoulder and said, "Don't worry you have us, you are not alone". That was nice for Michael to say that. A year before when Bob and his family had visited us, he could tell that Papa was declining, and Bob said, "Don't worry mamma, you have us". It was nice to hear these words. Just recently Marilou said, "I wish I had spent more time with Papa, taking him more often to lunch." I know we all wished we had spent more time, if we had just known. Dave had promised me an additional 5 years of his life with me. Marilou kept saying to go out with other people. I wanted to spend every minute with Dave. I knew in how badly shape he was. Marilou kept saying for me to retire. I couldn't. I talked with Dave about it and Dave told me:" Don't retire, if I die at least you have your job to hang on and you like teaching, like I did. Wait till you are 70 and then retire and we will travel."(Good plan). I told Dave if I died first, I was not worried because he would have been taken care of, and I had a better life insurance coverage that he had.

When Marilou moved the chair from outside where Dave used to sit, because it was upsetting Jo, my neighbor, I did not tell her that chair was a comfort for me, because while I am cutting the grass I could still see him waving at me smiling with his, as we called it, silly grin.

One of the hardest parts was going thru his clothes. When Bob was here he had helped me with some, but later I had to go through all of his clothes, pack them and donate them. I was talking with my friend Jan about it and she told me that when her mother had died, her father could not bring himself to clear the closet. So her and her children had gone to the house to help and take care of it. Jo, my neighbor just told me that it took her 5 years before she could go thru her son's clothes. He had been killed when he was 19 years old. There were many tears and heart breaking moments. I kept some of his favorite yellow shirts and his housecoat. It is like part of you is being destroyed. I have some good days but mostly bad days, when I feel my heart almost popping out from my chest. I talk do Dave and try to calm myself down. My friend Bev said, she can see her mother going thru the same process when her father would die (he is 85 years old), but she also told me the closeness of the family is what keeps the living person going on. I make a point to call my friends. At least every two weeks, I call my friend Carla in Italy (a widow), my friend Rosetta and my brother. Just recently when I talked to Rosetta I found out that Ada's (Rosetta's sister) husband Romeo had died. Ada lives with her children and when her children went on vacation to France, Rosetta had her stay with her. Ada is 77 years old like my brother. I was so sorry to hear this news. I knew both of them very well.

This mother's day it was my first one without Dave writing me a poem, I read the one from last year; it is not the same. It was my first Valentine, my first birthday, my first Christmas without his presence, my first father's day without him. I was cutting the grass, and edging and I could not stop crying. Tears kept falling on my face. Thank goodness no one was in the yard. I cried for more than a half hour, thinking of the past father's days, which we always spent with the children. I watched the soccer games. Dave and I had become really involved in the games. We both loved it.

I love when Laura and Bob call me and we talk about frivolous things, and when Marilou calls to ask what I am doing. It keeps my mind off for few minutes.

I feel so alone, but I'm trying my best for everyone sake. Dave and I had talked about what would happen to me after he was gone. He told me to go to the Salvation Army and get a homeless person to move in with me, to keep me company. I know he was very worried about my future. We had made all kind of plans when I was going to retire. It is nice to make plans for the future. In Italy we have a saying "L'uomo propone e Dio dispone." Men make plans but it is up to God for these plans to be executed. Our lives are in God's hands. Our plans never materialized.

It has been a year since his death. Yesterday, I spent most of the time working outside, trimming, edging, till it rained. Marilou called to ask what I was doing. Bob called later, to see how I was doing. I did not tell them that I cried most of the morning. I felt so alone. I am sure it was also hard on Bob, Marilou, Alessandra, Laura, Michael, Alyssa and Sharayah. I went with my neighbors to church; Marilou and Alessandra met us there. Then we went to dinner. I wasn't very hungry. I was trying very hard not to cry. Marilou and Alessandra went home; I went back to my home. It was raining very hard, maybe a message from Dave. I called Jan; I knew she was very worried about me. She kept asking, "Are you all right?" No reason to worry her. I watched the Olympic, and fell asleep, watching it. Finally, I woke up and went to bed. I talked with Dave, as I do every night.

I have lost my father, my mother and Dave. I keep seeing his face, while he was dying. I cannot take that image out of my mind, and probably never will.

I was talking to my brother about my feelings and he said to me "Rosaria, remember an old Neapolitan saying, "che vuoi fa', tira a campa'" (nothing you can do about it, just keep on living).

I miss Dave very much. I keep thinking of his last words to me, "I love you" and he kissed my hand.

Death leaves a heartache

no one can heal.

Love leaves a memory

no one can steal

Gone,

yet not forgotten although we are apart,

Your spirit lives within me, forever in my heart

# CHAPTER 2

## YOUR 55 ½ YEAR BIRTHDAY
## (David Wills)

Your half birthday is the answer,
To my being cured from prostate cancer.
So every birthday counts as two,
'Cause I'll be here much longer with you.
Enjoy our time and always laugh,
And celebrate on birthdays and the half.
While we age just half as much,
And we get younger with every touch.
Remember give thanks to heaven above,
For all our years and for all our love

As Always,
Dave

# CHAPTER 3

## Respite

There's a poor old man in a hospital bed
Stranded in the center of a dying sea
The sea is white and the bedstead iron
And the cost of dying free.
The sick old man doesn't want to die
And go to only God knows where
But he knows he can't only
Lie in bed
And exhale
His blood
And
Air.
This only man is only fifty-six
Not even the promised age
But with all the new and the wonderful drugs
Maybe he can turn a brand new and hopeful page
But no, it chews, and munches and eats
And the old man goes down and down
Whole family visits one last time,
The old man thinks with a frown,

*Rosaria M. Wills*

Why am I in a place like this
Instead of someone else?
Why they don't find something for me,
Without it I can
Not go—
My God
This old man is
This old man
Isn't

# CHAPTER 4

## OH, SAY CAN YOU SEE?
## (David Wills)

Francis, I know it's not light yet
And the sun won't rise for an hour,
But still with the rockets and flashes there
Keep a watch over by the tower

All yesterday we watched our banner
Waving in the rockets' red glare,
But now it's dark, but becoming light.
See if our flag is flying there.

Look, the British ships in theh arbor here
Are not firing their cannon any more,
But seem to be raising their sails
And moving away from shore.

See Francis, there a sun's ray shines
And confirms what we hoped all night
The American Flag is standing tall
And defies the British might.

I know our Washington Militia first stood,
Fired once, then broke and fled.
But at Baltimore they turned and began to fight
And how the British bled.

They gathered here at Fort McHenry
And the Great Revolution won,
Which guaranteed the rights and freedom
To every American daughter and son.

Old Glory is still there, standing tall.
And showing its red and white and blue,
Proclaiming our liberty to the whole wide world
And honoring our heroes true.

Long live the land the Revolution has made,
At the mountains let the word ring true,
From sea-to sea and border to border
God bless the Red, White and Blue

# CHAPTER 5

## MOTHER'S DAY 2002
## TRENTASETTE
## (By David Womack Wills)


I really don't mean to bug you
I surely would rather just hug you
Mother's Day is here again
My love and congratulations both I send.

Take the gifts, use them I say
To create at school a big display
I hope we make another thirty-seven
Unless I leave and go to heaven

But still I'll stay and wait for you
Because our love is so very true.
If I get there first, I'll sit and wait
Remember hon, we've got a date.

# CHAPTER 6

## ELEVEN YEARS LATER

It was about time for me to return to Italy and see my brother and some of my friends. I needed something that would pull me out of my sadness.

In February I purchased my ticket. Unfortunately there was not a direct flight. I had to change plane in Detroit. This was the first time that I would be travelling alone. My Dave had always been with me and when I went to New York, Marilou came with me. I had planned to spend two weeks with my brother in Velletri, one week with my friend Rosetta and one week with my friend Carla, a friend that I had never met. (In 1999 I had gone to the Poggi store to purchase some Armani. Some had to be shipped to Florida. I started buying more staff from the store, many also for my daughter and my granddaughter. Carla was in charge of the bookkeeping, so we started communicating thru E-mail, we exchanged pictures, and soon we became friends. She was a widow; her husband had died of cancer ten years before. She had a son named David, a niece Valentina and her sister Laura. We had E-mailed and called each other for the past ten years and we were dying to finally meet).

My trip started on the 23rd of June. I was extremely nervous. Marilou took me to the airport; I left with a heavy heart. I was lucky that they had a seat available in first class, and here I was in first class. Certainly it was more comfortable than coach. A man was sitting next to me. He went to sleep after about 4 beers.

We landed in Detroit, a hostess, who saw me so nervous, helped me thru custom and also to get to the other plane. I was lucky to sit next to a lady, travelling with her husband, her mother and daughter, who were very nice, and we started talking away. She could not sleep and I couldn't either. I was never able to sleep on planes, Dave instead as soon as he was on the plane he would fall asleep, holding my hand.

A little rough voyage, the pilot kept talking, talking. We landed in Rome, Italy. My new found friend helped me find my suitcases, the belt at the airport had broken and they were suitcases everywhere. Thank goodness Marilou had told me to put a ribbon on the suitcase so I could find it. They all seemed the same, and the same color.

My brother, Mimmo, was supposed to meet me at the airport. I did not see him; I did have his cell number so I called. He was upstairs instead of downstairs. He came down with his wife Rosaria. (Mimmo and Rosaria had fought for years, they never got along, and she did not particularly like my family. She could never stand my mother).

We met, we hugged, I was so happy to see my brother after so many years, he had of course aged like I had, but he still looked the same to me. We got in the car, he was getting lost, and Rosaria kept yelling where to go. I was hoping for Rosaria to become like a sister to me. We had talked on the phone many times and she was always pleasant.

We finally find the highway. Velletri is about one hour from Rome. I was looking around, remembering the times that I had come with my Dave.

We finally arrived at his house. I was very tired, it had been a long trip, but because of the six hours difference, I was trying to stay awake, so that I could get back on track.

The first four days at Mimmo and Rosaria's house were great. We visited the villas, went to a museum (my brother and I only, Rosaria would not come). Then we went every day to the market to buy food. I paid many times. Then the following times I bought dessert for all of us every day. My brother told me how unhappy he was with his wife, kept telling me that she was crazy. He remembered his old girlfriend Lilly over and over and his friend Domenico Mazzoni. I had come to Italy to talk about me, my loneness without Dave, instead I ended up just listening and listening.

We talked about the good old days, Rosaria prepared our dinner, and she seemed very nice.

We had made plans to go to Rome to see the Vatican, the Coliseums and the Trevi'fountain, but first Mimmo had a commitment with the Carabinieri. It was the last week for the undergraduate from the military school to leave, and since he had retired, they were expected to be at the graduation. I was looking forward to it. I had never seen one. I should have known something was wrong when Rosaria said she would not be going because there were never that many people and she preferred to stay home. We went to the Carabienieri's farewell. The stage was overcrowded. At the reception I met a nice Lieutenant Colonel. We talked for a while; it was nice to talk with someone without being interrupted.

I went with my brother to his eye surgery, Rosaria was mad so she did not come. Afterwards we went where my brother spends most of his time at his office, we brought some food, ate. Rosaria called, my brother told her we were still at the clinic, and that we will be late.

That evening she fixed some food, and there was hair in it, it made me sick to my stomach, but I did not say anything.

Every time we said we had met someone, she had to top us, don't matter what. She informed us again that she would not be going with us to Rome; she did not like to walk, and to be sure not to bother her from 2 p.m. to 4p.m., because at that time she rested.

Mimmo and I would take long walks together. He remembered the past, I just listened. I noticed that Rosaria was getting less and less friendly. I tried to agree with her and stay out of trouble. At one point I asked Mimmo if it would probably be better if I stayed at a Hotel, but my brother said no.

They fought continually, every time my brother would say something she will call him stupid, and yell. I was getting very uncomfortable. I stayed on the computer most of the times. She did not like that. Everyday I went for long walks and met very nice people.

One time she sent Mimmo and I to buy a white pizza (is a pizza bare of everything, and then you can fix it as you like it.) We walked and looked every where but there was none. When we came back and told her she called us liars and did not cook. I made myself and Mimmo a sandwich.

She hated everyone in the building, I would say hello, and she will get very angry. I guess not matter what I did I was always wrong.

I was supposed to go to Salerno, to Rosa's house for one week. So I called her to make arrangements. Unfortunately she had entered a TV competition called the "Velona" and she was not going to be home. She offered to give me the keys to her house, but as I told her what could I do without a car, just staying at her house? I knew I could not stay with Mimmo and Rosaria, so I first E-mailed, then called Carla and asked her to find me a hotel room for one week, and one week I would stay with her. Carla did not want to hear about a hotel, she firmly said, "Rosaria, you are going to stay with me two weeks, let me know at what time you will arrive either by plane or train."

I thanked her and made arrangements to go to Florence by train. I gave Carla the time and the day.

In the meantime the saga in my brother's house continued. I was showing my brother how to use U-tube so he could listen to his music. She came to the room, and said in a harsh voice. "Stop talking and playing on the computer you to, I have to rest." My brother and I apologized, and closed the door, so she would not hear us.

My brother kept asking me to talk with his son, Robert, how erratic Rosaria was. I did not want to interfere; I tried to buy time by saying that I would E-mail or call when I got home.

Then hell broke loose. We were watching the Soccer championship and Brazil and Holland were playing. My brother and I decided to cheer for Holland. Rosaria screaming said, "You are a bunch of racist, I am cheering for Brazil." I asked her if she knew what racist meant, since it did not make any sense, and she answered," I know everything". So all thru the game she screamed and cheered for Brazil. Brazil lost and Holland won.

The finals were the next day. My brother and I sat to watch it; she sat next to us, and kept changing channel. Mimmo asked, "Can you please stop changing channel so we can watch the game."

"I don't want to watch it, if you want, go with your sister in the kitchen and watch it on the little TV (The TV was about 9 inches)."

We got up and went to the kitchen to watch it, while she kept screaming and talking in a loud voice in the other room. I guess she did not realize that in soccer you do not listen but watch the game. It was a good game. Holland won, we went back in the living room, she was laying down in her underwear.

Mimmo and I went to Rome, saw the Coliseum, The Vatican City, Fountain of Trevi. I was trying not to cry. We sat at the Coliseum and he kept thinking about the past, and how sad he was and how bad his life was. I offered him to come with me to the States, and stay with me . . . he said no. He has prostate's problems. They will not operate because he is too old. That is social medicine for you.

The next day we went to a restaurant with their friends. She was making plans to go with her girlfriend to go some place on a Sunday, I said, "I thought you don't like to go out on Sunday." She did not answer.

A man approached us, Mimmo knew him, and he started talking, then he left.

When we finished and went home, Rosaria said to Mimmo, "Tell that man that I do not want him to come to our table at the restaurant, he spits on the food."

I said "He did not, he seemed nice."

Again yelling (that was the only way she would communicate), "Mimmo, do you understand, no more this guy." My brother promised to talk to him, but I knew he had no intention on doing it.

During my two weeks stay, she never changed my sheets, only my pillow case once and with complains. I went to the Laundromat to wash my clothes; she did have a washing machine that she rarely used.

She hated when I took showers. She told me that she only bathed once a month, and then she washed daily. I guess she did not use deodorant because her smell made me gag. I took short showers every two, three days, and she made me feel very guilty.

When sometimes, we will be talking about politics, and I said something about Obama, she would scream, "I love Obama," and when I tried to explain his shortcoming, she would scream again, "I love him, and that is it".

I wear a necklace that has our Lady of the Rosary medallion, a horse' shoe and a horn, (I have worn this since I was 10 years old). She looked at my necklace and said, "This is a disgrace for you wearing Our Lady with good luck charms."

"I have been wearing for years, and certainly I will keep wearing it till I die, or maybe take it with me to the grave."

I kept quiet, in fact I tried very hard not to talk, just listen, because anytime I started a conversation she would stop me and kept on talking about some thing else. I really think there is something seriously wrong with her, mentally.

It was few days before my final departure. I offered to take them to a restaurant. She refused, so we went to a bar to have ice cream, or whatever else they wanted. We left, everything seemed fine. We sat at the bar. She ordered some sort of drink, Mimmo and I an ice cream. Then Mimmo started talking about the past, his past girlfriends. I was sitting there, till Rosaria jumped up from the seat, and said, "Yeh, sure the past, then go and leave me alone". This was all done in a screaming voice. It was quite embarrassing. I suggested I pay and leave.

I went in the bar to pay, they started walking, Rosaria screaming and so did my brother, how unhappy he was, that he wanted to talk with the lawyer for a divorce. She kept screaming go ahead, and then so she did not have to listen to him, she placed her fingers in her ears, and sang "La, La, La . . .". I was truly embarrassed. Everyone was looking and laughing. She almost got ran over by a car because she could not hear the horn. My brother grabbed her and tried to strangle her, I stopped him, and pulled him away, while she kept screaming, "Go ahead, kill me, and go to jail. See if I care."

Finally we arrived at home. We walked inside, still both of them screaming. I tried to calm them down, but not succeeding. My brother slept on the couch, he said normally sleeps in the room where I was sleeping. I felt so guilty. I was so scared of what she could do. So that night I placed a chair against the door, so I could hear her coming. I couldn't sleep, I kept praying to God to let the last few days go by really fast and I cried all night.

The next day, I talked to her, suggesting to maybe see a counselor or a priest, since both Mimmo and her were so religious. She yelled, "Well, you should have done something yesterday, you are like your brother, useless."

I answered, "I saved your life from being strangled, and run over by a car."

I walked away, barely talking to each other. My day was finally coming when I could leave. I was counting the hours.

Rosaria does not drive (because she is too nervous), she does not use the computer. She does not ride elevator, because someone long time ago got stuck in an elevator. She has a 5th grade education, but apparently she knows everything.

The morning of my departure came. My brother and I were ready to go. Rosaria said "Well, you and your mother are terrible, so is Mimmo, don't you ever come back to my house. You have spent too much time on the computer with your brother. You have not swept the house."

I had cleaned my room, washed dishes and pans every day. I had not swept the whole house, because I did not use the whole house. Then she started saying, "Your mother was a horrible person, I slaved for her every day when she was here." That was 35 years ago.

I said, "Stop bad mouthing my mother, she is dead, but she had powers, she was a witch and has powers to punish you if you keep bringing up her name." (Of course I was lying)

I thanked her for her wonderful hospitality, said Bye, Bye and left.

Mimmo and I left. On the way to the train station my brother kept begging me to call Robert and tell him how crazy his mother was. I promised I would, but I had no intention to do it.

We arrived to the train station for Florence; he said if I came back we will have to meet in Rome. He had tears in his eyes, he looked so old. I begged him again to come with me, or join me later. He said "Who knows." We hugged and then he left.

My train trip was okay, I kept thinking of the miserable two weeks, except the times that I had spent with Mimmo and seeing the places that I had been before. I missed not going to Naples.

I was lucky that a young man on the train helped me with the suitcases. There were so heavy because I had purchased many crossword puzzles books. (Almost 12 pounds in weight). I arrived at the station and went the wrong way, and then I turned around and saw Carla. (I had told her what I would be wearing).

I was surprised on how tiny Carla was, red hair and blue eyes. We hugged, we were so happy to see each other. She had a car with A/C, she helped me with the suitcases, and arrived at her house. An apartment, with elevator . . . We talked, talked . . . I did not say anything about my horrendous experience in Velletri. She had to work, and told her not to worry . . . I will go with her in the morning, go around the town, then meet her for lunch, and in the afternoon go home.

She refused to let me pay for anything including when we went out to eat. I finally said, "Carla, I am taking you to the manicure and pedicure, I am buying lunch everyday, and you better not say no."

While Carla was at work, I would go around and re-visited the places that I had been with my David, Palazzo Pitti, La Signoria, the gardens. I would sit on the steps of Piazza della Signoria, a man would be playing a guitar, beautiful music. He was Russian. He would sell his Cd. I did not buy one, but I spent hours listening to the music. Behind the Duomo there was a museum with air conditioner. There were beautiful statues. I saw one that looked like the Pieta, but a man was holding Jesus. I asked the person in charge who this man was, he told me, that was Michelangelo holding

Jesus, Michelangelo's Pieta. He had planned to place it as tombstone on his grave. They were four of these statues, one also in Milan, and Rome. It was very impressive. Then I decided one day to go to the Belle Arti Museum to see again the David. The line was enormous, it was hot. Next to me in line were two young girls, and behind me a young man. We started talking, all three were Americans, and where studying arts. I send one of the girls to ask how much longer, she came back, saying probably two more hours . . . it was getting pretty hot. I finally went to the entrance to ask if there was any way to go in . . . he said, go ahead, and there is when I said in Italian, "These three people are my children, I cannot leave my children out." He looked at me, and said, "Go, ahead with your children." We went in, we laughed, and kept playing around, the David was as usual astounding, We stayed for a while, left, and said our goodbyes. The young man wrote music and gave me a CD. I have not listened to it yet.

Time was going by fast. In the evening Carla and I would go to the ice cream parlor. Many times, with her family, Valentina, Davide, and Laura, to eat at the pizzeria, she refused to have me pay.

I am an avid reader of Twlight, which takes place in Tuscany. I asked my friend to go to Volterra, where the movie supposedly had taken place. She drove; we arrived at Volterra, a beautiful medieval city. I was looking around for the Duomo where the final scene in the movie takes place, but there was no Duomo, finally after walking around for hours, I asked one of the vendors, "Where is the Duomo, with the last scene from the movie New Moon." He knew what I was talking about and told me, "They could not do the scene here, because there is no Duomo, so they filmed the rest of the movie in Montepulciano, a city near by."

We were too tired and decided to leave. I had two wonderful weeks. Her family treated me like part of their family, a typical Italian caring family. She had placed a ventilator in my room so I would be comfortable, and yes she took showers every day so would I.

Time went by too fast. She took me to the airport; we hugged, promised to see each other again, me trying to convince her to come to see me with all her family in Florida. The plane in Florence was late; we sat in the plane for two hours. I arrived in Rome, sat again for two hours in the plane. Finally I left for Atlanta, to change planes for Orlando, again two more hours in Atlanta. The trip coming back took almost 12 hours. I was exhausted. Jo and Bud, my neighbors came to pick me up, since Marilou and Alessandra had gone to a competition. Back home, back to my memories, but now I could add additional memories.

I called my brother, I told him I was not going to write to Roberto about his mother, and again invited him to move with me. He never will, they will be at each other throat till one of them dies.

Now I call my brother on his cell phone, so that Rosaria does not know. Mimmo told me that when I call him at home she gives him hell for the whole week. So I try E-mail, and call him on the cell phone. My only brother, my only family of what is left.

# CHAPTER 7

## BREAKING NEWS

"A man named Jamie Smith, age 28 went missing on Friday, August 13, 2010. He was last seen walking up to the elevators of McKenzie Towers, in Savannah, Georgia.

According to Mr. Darel, Jamie Smith never checked into the hotel. If you have seen this man please call 1-800-555-5555."

Dustin and Katie were very shocked by what they had heard on the news. Their best friend was missing.

"We have to find him". Katie thought.

"We have to find him as soon as possible." Dustin told Katie eagerly.

Katie thought about their chances of actually finding their friend. The chances were slim but they had to try. The news said that he was last seen at McKenzie Towers, which is right by his apartment, so why would he go there?

Katie pondered about this before Dustin spoke, "I think we should run by his apartment and see if there are any clues that he might have left."

Katie did not have to say anything for Dustin to know that she agreed.

Katie just nodded and they left for Jamie's house.

Once they arrived at Jamie's apartment, Katie lifted the door mat to get the extra key he always kept there. Dustin walked in first, being the protector. The first room Katie searched was the bathroom. Dustin first searched Jamie's bedroom.

"Katie! You might want to come see this!" Dustin yelled to Katie from Jamie's room. Katie ran into the room to find Dustin sitting on the bed holding a picture.

"What is it?," Katie asked in a scared tone.

"It's a picture of Jamie . . . with . . . blood all over it. Look at the mirror." Dustin said in a whisper.

Katie did not want to look but she did not have a choice. Katie was out of breath. On the mirror were words written in blood. There was also a signature that she could not read because of the smeared blood.

The words read, "This is Jamie's blood. I don't think you want him to loose anymore of it. If you want your friend back you need to come and find him. You already know the building, now you need the room and level. Your first clue is number 2. Go to DM to find your answer."

Katie just stared at the mirror in shock. Then she started crying. Katie, the 27 years old, who never cried, cried for her dear friend Jamie.

"Jaime is hurt. They took his blood to write with it. We have to find him fast."

Dustin just patted her back to comfort her as he thought of a plan.

"Ok first we need to go to McKenzie Towers and find this DM person. Also we have to figure out what the number 2 stands for." Dustin explained to Katie as he read the number off a piece of paper. Dustin and Katie were running thru their plan on the way to McKenzie Towers.

"We need to get our answer to DM and see where we will go from there. He will probably give us another clue." Katie suggested.

Dustin nodded as they went through the spinning doors of McKenzie Towers.

Dustin and Katie walked over to the nearest table to figure out what the number 2 meant.

"Who is DM? Let's ask that man over there."

Katie and Dustin walked over the man sitting behind the front desk.

"Excuse me, sir. Do you know a man with the initials DM?" Katie asked scared to know the answer.

"My initials are DM. Do you have the answer I am looking for?"

Dustin rummaged through his pocket and soon found the piece of paper that had the answer on it.

"Here you go, Sir, I have number 2" he said.

"Here is your next clue." Said DM. The clues were 13, 0 and 8.

"Now, go, and figure out which is the floor and which one is the room number. There you will find your destiny. Have fun brats." DM told them and walked away.

"Did he just call us brats?" Katie asked in a shocked tone. Dustin nodded and said eagerly. "Let's go find the room and the floor."

"I find number 13, what about you?" Dustin asked.

"Mine is 138. I don't think there is a 138 floor so that must be the room number, and 13 must the floor. I have never seen a hotel with a 13th floor. It is bad luck."

Katie's voice trembled as she spoke.

"Let's move then." Dustin almost yelled as they went to the elevators on the other side of the hotel. Katie pushed the up bottom, and two of them waited patiently while the elevator came down very slowly. The elevator bell sounded. The doors slid open very slowly and a man the size of the Empire Sate Building came out and grabbed them. "Ms. Molly does not want to wait any longer for you brats. Go meet your destiny."

The big man pressed 13 as the doors closed us into the tight space; it was only a couple of seconds.

Once the door opened the big man pushed us down the long corridor to a cream colored door with a key slot. The number was 1308.

"Open the door," the man behind them told Dustin. He did and the man pushed Katie and Dustin inside. It was very dark. No light could be seen through the curtains in front of the sliding glass door. The beds were made from as much as Katie could see through the darkness. There were two figures on a chair in front of them, one sitting and one laying on the floor.

"Well there you are. You are finally here. Here is your friend." Molly said as she kicked the figure on the floor. Dead.

"Now it is your turn," Molly said getting up.

"No . . . ." Katie and Dustin yelled in unison . . . .

What was going to happen?

Was it just a bad dream or reality!!!!!

# CHAPTER 8

## THE CASE OF THE MISSING PEPPER

It was a bright Saturday afternoon in the vegetable garden. The land was owned by farmer Mary who worked in the garden for hours and hours every day. She had a strong passion for gardening, but her favorite vegetable to grow was pepper. On that Saturday afternoon, she discovered something that disturbed her.

"Oh, no!," said farmer Mary. "One of my red peppers is missing!"

One of her other peppers overheard Mary and became curious. This pepper's name was Nanny, Nanny Pepper and he was determined to find his lost pepper friend. Nanny called a group meeting of all the pepper's in the garden.

Nanny said, "I overheard farmer Mary crying out that one of the peppers is missing. Now does anyone know who this pepper may be?"

There was no answer, just a crowd of mumbling and confused peppers. Then one brave pepper stood up and said, "I think I know who the missing pepper is."

Nanny declared, "Great! Which pepper is missing?"

The little pepper said, "I believe her name is Carol. She said she was going to go to the house last night to water herself, and then she never came back to the pot."

The anxious crowd gasped simultaneously. "Oh, my!" said Nanny Pepper. "We must start searching immediately!"

The peppers all agreed to start the search for Carol, for she could be anywhere in the garden by now.

The peppers broke into groups.

"Carol, Carol pepper!" They all cried out. They never got an answer. Nanny's group of valiant peppers was stumped. One of the peppers, Penny, suggested. "How about we ask one of the crows?"

The group did not respond, "Come on guys", Penny persuaded. "I know it may be a little dangerous, but it is for Carol. Besides, some of the crows are really nice."

The rest of the group talked a little bit, then agreed. So the peppers ventured over to the crow zone. They all knew the crows would be over near the corn. When they got there, they heard many squeaks and squawks. Nanny stepped forward and said, "Hello crow! My name is Nanny Pepper, and Carol the pepper has gone missing. Have any of you seen her?"

The crows looked at each other and chatted. Then one crow came out and said, "Good afternoon peppers. My name is Cole crow, and I reckon' I have seen a lonesome pepper wondering around this neck of the garden late last night. What if I give you a clue?

If you have $4.00 and divide it between two people, how many dollars do you have for each person"

Nanny's group was confused. "I don't understand, Cole." Questioned Nanny.

"Well this clue tells you in what row of the garden I saw her."

Nanny understood the mission and said, "I see. Well thank you, Mister Cole for all of your help. I hope to see you all again. Bye."

Then the group was off again. They stopped when they reached an area of shade. Then Nanny began, "Now, what does this clue say,"

Another pepper said, "I know, it is number 2."

The group was thinking very hard. Then Nanny said, "Oh, I am stumped. Does anyone here know what it means? We are in a bit of a hurry."

The group thought about the problem some more, then Peggy pepper said, "I got it. She is in row #2."

The whole group cheered and was so excited.

"Good work, Peggy," Nanny congratulated.

"Now let's go find Carol."

The group went on through the garden, searching for row 2.

"What row are we in?" asked Penny.

"Uh . . . I believe we are in row # 3." Peggy replied. "Look, there is row 2." declared Nanny.

The peppers ran to row 2, but when they looked, they saw nothing but baby potatoes.

"Carol!" they called, though they got no reply.

"Cole Crow told us she would be here." cried Patrick pepper.

"We must have patience. He saw Carol here hours ago. She could be anywhere by now. What if we ask that corn snake over there?" Nanny suggested.

"It's worth a shot." bellowed Penny.

"Then let's go guys." Patrick yelled.

They walked over to the snake and Nanny said, "Hello, I am Nanny Pepper, we are looking for our friend, have you seen her? She looks a lot like us. She has been missing since last night."

The corn snake hissed and slithered around. Then she finally said, "Hi, Greetingsss my friends. I am Sydney, the snake. I do believe I have ssseen your friend. The lassst place I saw her was, wait there is the clue. Find the square root of 4." Nanny was disappointed by the answer.

"Another riddle?" he asked.

"Yess . . . my dear, remember patience issss key."

Nanny took deep thought into this statement, "Alright, thank you so much Sydney snake. Bye, bye now."

The peppers were off again to solve another riddle.

"So", began Patrick. "What's the answer this time?"

Peggy pondered for a bit and then she said, "If I am not mistaken, Carol was last seen in . . . uhh . . . row 2?" The group waited in silence.

"Row 2, we were just there!" Penny reminded them. "Yes, well, let us go back and see if she is there." Nanny ordered.

So they headed back towards row 2. When they arrived they called, "Carol, Carol, Are you there Carol?" Still there was no answer. The group felt like that they had failed Carol. Then Patrick said, "Well, we can always try asking that rabbit over there."

The group agreed that it was worth a try. So when they got to the rabbit Nanny said, "Good afternoon stranger. I am Nanny Pepper and we are looking for one of our pepper friends, Carol. Have you happened to have seen her around?"

The rabbit thought and thumped his foot. Then he finally said, "Greetings, I am Ronald rabbit. I do actually recall seeing a pepper roaming around here. Yes, I think it was somewhere around here an hour ago. I saw her. Here is your clue. Find the first even number."

The group was getting angry hearing all these riddle. "Well, thank you Ronald rabbit for all your help. Bye."

Again the group went and took a seat. They all sighed, for they felt that this journey will never end.

"Ok, Peggy, can you solve this riddle?" Nanny said.

"Yes, yes, I can. Let' see here . . . ."

Peggy thought and thought and finally said, "How can this be right. It's row 2." "The group began to mumble and complain, and then Nanny said, "Quiet, We will go to row 2, again, Carol could be there, we are just not seeing her."

The group gave a large sigh and walked over to row 2.

"Ok," Nanny said, "We must go look through the row."

Everyone walked through yelling, "Carol, Carol pepper. Where are you Carol?"

The group again was not successful. They felt that they should give up.

Nanny then said, "Come on guys, what are we doing? We can do better than this. We are all family here, and families do not just give up on each other because they feel tired or that nothing is working. We need to fight till the very end for Carol. If you still want to find Carol Pepper with me say 'I'."

The whole group declared, "I".

"Then let's go find Carol," Nanny affirmed

The group decided to go to an animal that they knew would give them a knowledgeable answer. This would require waiting for the evening. The group of peppers waited and waited until they heard a sound of hope. "HOOT . . . HOOT . . . HOOT . . . HOOT." The peppers shook with excitement, for they knew Carol was to be found tonight.

"Good evening, Mr. Owl." Nanny said hopefully.

"I am Nanny Pepper and we are looking for our lost pepper friend. Have you happened to see a pepper today?"

The owl spun his head around and around and finally he said, "Salutations, my friends. My name is Oliver owl. I have seen your pepper friend. The other animals around the garden have been talking about you. I heard you have spoken to Cole crow, Sydney snake, Ronald the rabbit, and now me. So this makes 4 animals?"

Nanny said, "Yes, Mr. Oliver".

Oliver said in a low voice. "Your friend is in . . . ." Peggy then chimed in the conversation, "now, wait a minute already. I know this riddle off the top of my head. The answer is 2 again. We have looked in row 2 three times already, and she isn't in there."

Oliver owl said, "I know what the answer is my dear. Listen closely to what I say. All the answers you got were 2. You talked to 4 people, do you follow?"

The peppers all shook their heads in confusion, when Peggy said, "I get it. I know where Carol is. She is in row 8 right?" Oliver owl nodded in approval.

"Yes, good job Peggy? Now let's go find our friend." Nanny announced.

"Thank you so much Oliver owl."

The peppers ran as fast as they could to row 8. They were all filled with anxiety hoping Carol would be located there. When they arrived they called, "Carol, Carol are you there,?" then a small voice said, "over here, I'm over here!"

Nanny said. "Follow me."

They all ran to where they heard Carol's voice. Then they saw what they had been searching for all day. It was Carol pepper, stuck in the wet soil of a carrot pot.

"Carol we are so glad to see you." They hollered with joy.

"Thank you all so much. I have been worried sick that I was never going to get out of this wet pot. I was going to water myself when I decided to take a shortcut through the carrot pots. I had forgotten that they were freshly watered and landed right into the soil. I cannot wait to go back to row 5, the pepper section."

Nanny stepped forward and said, "We are so glad to have you back Carol. Come on, let's go back to row 5."

Carol and the rest of the gang made it back safely to row 5. The other search groups were already there. Everyone was so relieved to have Carol back safe and sound. They celebrated Carol's return all night long.

The next morning, farmer Mary came out to do her count of vegetables. When she got to the peppers, she had one more than yesterday, "Oh, my," she hollered. "My pepper has come back."

She picks it up and takes it to the kitchen.

# CHAPTER 9
## ONE DARK AND STORMY NIGHT

One dark and stormy night one of Angelina Jolie's recently adopted children was kidnapped out of her bed. When Brad Pitt did his morning head count, he noticed that 1 kid was missing. Monroe the butler came into the room holding a ransom note.

"Sir, you have a ransom note for one of your children by the name of Stephanie," Monroe said.

"Oh, that's where she went," Brad commented.

"Be quiet, Brad; give me the note," Angelina commanded.

The note read: "I have your kid, Stephanie. Give me $1,000,000 or you will never see your little Asian baby again".

Angelina dropped the note, and pulled $1,000,000 out of her purse.

"This is just pocket money."

Monroe handed her another note.

This one read:

"Put money in Monroe's pocket."

Brad looked at Angelina, took the money, put it in Monroe's pocket and said, "Get little Suzy back!"

Little Suzy got up from the table.

"Daddy, I'm right here, it's Stephanie who is missing," Suzy whined.

"I knew that." Brad said shaking his head.

They called the police and an hour later a large Russian officer with a mole on her chin came to the door.

"Hello, I Helga," she said with a Russian accent. "What is the problem?"

"Our baby was stolen from her bed, our poor little Sophie." Brad cried.

"Stephanie!" Sophie yelled at her father.

"Oh, yeah," Brad said while dropping to his knees. "Poor little . . . uhm . . . Stephanie."

"Get off the floor," Helga ordered, while lifting Brad off the floor by his ear. Angelina walked in and gasped at the sight of her husband being harassed by a he-she in uniform.

"Put him down, another child just went missing," Angelina screamed.

"What is kid's name?", Helga asked.

"George," Angelina replied.

"NOO, not Greg!" Brad screamed.

"Brad, go make the kids some food while I talk with Helga."

"How much?"

"1,000,000 dollars"

"Isn't that a lot?"

"No, we have 15 kids."

A few weeks went by and they're down to their last baby and last 100 million.

"Brad, let's just forget about those kids and adopt more."

"But what if Jeffrey steals our monkey?"

"No, not the monkey; we have to keep the monkey safe no matter what, I love it."

"Me too Angie, me too; I love him 101%."

"Yes, me too, but isn't that cruel to leave our kids with some ransom man by the name of Jeffrey Monroe?"

"I don't really care, I mean all they did was whine," Brad complained.

"I know, honey, but that's what kids do when you can't remember their names."

"Seriously, well it's not my fault, there is just so many of them," Brad whined.

Monroe came running into the room.

"You are so rude!"

"What would make you say that, Monroe?"

"I am the one who stole your children, Jeffrey-Monroe. Now give me 12 millions dollars."

Angelina looked in her purse, pulled out her checkbook, and wrote a check for 13 million dollars.

"12 millions for the kids, and 1 million for the wonderful babysitting."

She gave Jeffrey the check, and he gave her all the kids back and to this day, Brad still does not remember his kid's names.

# CHAPTER 10

## THE EQUATION SLASHER

It was a dreary day in Longwood, Florida. The equation slasher was sharpening her pencil, she was going to math to slash the equation. She walked into the class, and no one suspected a thing. $2E-6=7+E$ was mysteriously written on the board. The teacher, Mrs. Brown did not know why there was an equation on the board because they were doing graphing. Then Mrs. Brown got an idea. "Well since the equation is already on the board, let's solve it."

Gabe raised her hand and walked to the front of the class and solved the equation, $E=13$. Suddenly Kelsey's hand shot up, "Oh my Gosh, look." Emma had a newly sharpened pencil in her neck. "She has been . . . slashed." Francesca screamed.

The next day the class and the slasher walked into Mrs. Brown room. History repeated itself; there was another equation, mysteriously written on the board. $4c-10=9+3c$.

"Oh, look, another equation. Who wants to solve it today?"

James raised his hand, "Me".

He ran up to the board, grabbed a black marker, and effortlessly solved the equation. "It is $C=19$".

There was a shriek from behind him. James turned around only to find Sydney with a pencil in her neck. James threw up and fainted.

Day by day, more equations appeared on the board, and one by one a different student was slashed. Brianna, Monroe, Brett, Teddy, Megan the first, Megan the second, Nicola . . . and so on.

Each day the ambulance came but they could not figure out the cause of death . . . Somehow . . . Now only seven students remained.

The next day, those seven remaining students entered the classroom. Crash!!. "Who dropped the calculator?" shouted Mrs. Brown.

"I did," said Gabriel.

Mrs. Brown snatched the calculator out of Gabe's hand but not too quickly to see the equation 2J-9=J+9.

James knew what was going on by now and he also knew he was next, Gabe understood that he had to solve it, and as soon as he pressed 'equal' and J=18 popped up on the screen, James shrieked. There was a pen in James neck and he was dead.

The next day, the rest of the class had enough. They called in . . . THE STITCHERS.

They came with special equipment to be used to detect the slasher. "Beep, Beep, Beeep!!!

"OMG, I can't believe this!" Jade screeched.

"The slasher is . . . is . . . Maria!!!???!!!"

Everyone screamed simultaneously. "Yes, Yes. It was I, Maria. I hear you all talk about how quiet I am and all that junk." She yelled in raging anger. "Well, who is the quiet one now!!!!. All those classmates I slashed! That's who!!"

"Maria, calm down!" Madison said, "It's not all that serious you know. Ha-ha, but I am pretty serial about. This is not time for jokes; they did not deserve what you did to them."

"Yes, they did!" Maria replied.

"This ends now, you serial slasher." Jade yelped.

She quickly ran over to the board wrote an equation. Emily yelled out the answer. All of a sudden, Maria began to get pelted with erasers her natural enemy.

It was over, the slasher was defeated, and all who was lost was brought back. How so?

Well that's another mystery in itself.

# CHAPTER 11

## THE CHASE

In Los Angeles, California, lives an undercover FBI agent. This agent goes by the name John Smith. John Smith is the FBI's top agent. He goes around solving many mysteries and crimes. On this particular night John is after a man who is suspected of robbing a local bank. The FBI thinks this man is going to a party on $4^{th}$ street, John plans on going to this party and trying to catch the suspected crook. This party is being held by a rich lawyer named Charles Castro. Charles is the $4^{th}$ world's richest man.

Charles and John have been buddies since college, where they both shared a dorm for their junior year. They both attended Westwood College. This particular criminal, whom John is looking for, has been a wanted man for many years for multiple reasons. He has been caught once before for auto theft. He did 4 years in prison. Now it appears that he has moved to bigger and better crimes. The suspect is attending this party along with his girlfriend and is supposed to arrive at the Castro household at about 7:30 P.M. John's plan is to attend the party then locate the suspect and then handcuff him and take him back to the FBI office for interrogation.

When John arrives at the party at 7:20 P.M. sharp he saw many sports cars and other vehicles of great value. He walked up the paved steps and knocked on the large door which seemed to tower over him. He could hear music and voices from inside. After about 30 seconds of waiting the large doors finally opened to reveal a lobby which was filled with people dancing and partying. John was greeted by Ilene, Charles's wife. John thanked Ilene and entered the house. John observed the crowds. He did not notice anything unusual, just people enjoying the party. John was carrying a picture of the suspected criminal just in case he forgot what the man looked like. It was now 7:28 P.M., then someone knocked at the door. John hurried over and found a spot where he could easily see the door. Ilene answered the door and sure enough it was the suspect. John looked at the man. He was about 6'1 with short brown hair. He was well groomed.

He walked in behind his girlfriend and thanked Ilene. The man then went off to another room. John asked Ilene about the man. Ilene said that this man went by the name Ryan Young. He was supposedly Charles's business partner.

John was not convinced. He still believed this man was guilty. He walked into the room where Ryan was standing. John just watched. Ryan looked up to John and made eye contact. He then returned to his girlfriend and said something which John did not hear. Ryan then started to jog out of the room and into a dimly lighted hallway. John followed a little bit behind. When John entered the hallway he was hit with the fresh scent of candles. John looked up and down the hallway and saw Ryan running down the left side. John chased after him; Ryan turned and ran into a room. He slammed the door shut and locked it. John pulled out his gun which he kept in a holster on his belt buckle all the times. He yelled for Ryan to open the door but there was no answer. He kicked the door in and pulled up his gun. He looked around but saw nothing. The room looked like a hotel room. When he entered the main part of the room he noticed an open balcony. He walked out and looked down but again saw nothing. Then all of the sudden two hands grabbed him. John was pushed up against the cold metal of the balcony. The man behind him squeezed at his waist. He struggled to get free from the grip of the mystery man but had no luck. A voice from behind him told him to remain still or else he was going over the edge. John nodded his head in agreement. He still had his gun out and had slipped it into his holster right as he was being grabbed. The man held onto John with a strong grip. He remained still as he was instructed. After about three minutes of this he began to think of a way out. He then thought of one. He grabbed the man at his waist and flipped him over his back until the man was hanging over the rail. When he looked down at him it was Ryan but that was not a surprise. He then pulled Ryan over the rail and laid him on the balcony floor. Put cuffs on the man and escorted him down the hall again. All of a sudden Ryan bolted back down the same hallway except in the opposite direction. He went into another room and locked the door. John did not want to ruin another one of Charles doors so he decided to just pick the lock. He looked at the key hole. It was about 2 inches wide. This was to John's advantage because this type of lock could be easily opened with a hairpin. He pulled a hairpin out of his pocket and slid it into the key hole. He turned and pushed until the door slid open. He walked in quietly. He looked around the dark room. He saw Ryan slither under the bed.

He went over to the bed and pulled Ryan out. Then he grabbed him by the arms and dragged him back into the hallway. He took him to his car and to the FBI office. John's chief thanked him for his good work and then sent him on his way. When John arrived at home he walked into the kitchen and made himself a sandwich and then sat down and watched ESPN. Another good day at work for John.

# CHAPTER 12

## CLEOPATRA'S TREASURES

Eight year old Miranda Delmonte, lived in the United Kingdom and she loved to hear stories from her father. Jonathan, her father had told her stories ever since she was a little girl. Her father would tell her a story every night and it was always new and exciting. He told her stories day and night twenty four seven.

Jonathan's stories were always about Egyptian history, myths, and even tales. His mother was full Egyptian, making him half Egyptian. Jonathan cared very much about his family's history and loved learning more and more about it, but his favorite part was to share it with his daughter who he loved with all his heart.

The last few nights Jonathan had been telling Miranda about Cleopatra. As he tells her about Cleopatra's history and success, Miranda's eyes grow wide with astonishing excitement, as she listens carefully to every word that flows gently and mysteriously out of her father's mouth. But what really gets Miranda is the treasure and gifts that Cleopatra left behind when she died. They still had not been found it. Jonathan told Miranda that the treasures were still hidden somewhere in the Sahara Desert.

"I'll find it daddy, just wait, I will find the treasure once I graduate from college," said Miranda.

Her father shut off the lights and she fell asleep dreaming about all the treasures.

Fifteen years later, when Miranda is nineteen years old, she had just enrolled at the Oxford University of Literature. Her goal was to graduate with a degree. One day as usual she grabbed her textbooks and two binders and ran to class so she wont' be late. But then all of the sudden her phone rings and it is her father. She answers and the only thing she hears is, "Help!, Miranda. Some guys are in the house stealing all of my books and maps of Egypt."

After she heard her dad say that on the phone, the phone goes to a dial tone and Miranda is frozen on her track. Miranda cannot believe what she had just heard and she feels a huge knot in her throat and she is extremely worried. Many thoughts are running through her head. She wonders what should she do, should she call the cops?

Miranda decided to go check out her father's house. When she arrives, the house is totally trashed and there is no one there, the house is dead silent. She starts to get worried and panics. Miranda searches the house to look for clues of who could have done all this damage. As she is looking around, she steps ever so lightly because there is broken glass every where; she walks into the den where her father kept all his important books and maps of everything. She stares around the room and there is not one Egyptian history book or even a map. But Miranda's eyes come across a piece of paper attached to the top of her father's chair, she begins to read.

"Whomever it may concern. We have Jonathan Delmonte and you might be wondering who is writing this. Well, we are gravediggers from Egypt. We have heard that Jonathan is an expert on Ancient Egyptian History. We are after Cleopatra's treasures. You also might be thinking 'is Jonathan safe or in any type of danger'. The answer is YES. If he does not tell us where to find the missing treasure we will leave him in the Sahara desert with no food or water, and protection. Do not call the police it will only make matters worse. If you wish to find Jonathan go to these coordinates 6 degrees north and 12 degrees east. Good luck . . ."

Miranda was completely shocked; she knew that she had to help her dad. She remembered always fantasizing about finding those treasures. She knew now that this was her one and only chance. Miranda was ready to go to Egypt and save her father and find Cleopatra's treasure. She packed her bags, got some maps, and headed off not knowing what was in store for her. She got on the plane and she just thought and imagined what was going to happen.

While she was on the plane she read some of the Egyptian books and she learned a lot about it that she never knew before. She figured that the treasure might be at the coordinates 10 degrees east and 20 degrees north. She decided on a plan.

1. find a way of transportation around the desert.
2. Find the treasure
3. Save her dad.

Miranda looked down at her list and she got a rush of confidence, she thought in her head "I can do this, I can do this, I can do it."

After the plane ride ended she got off and it was hot.

Miranda decided that she would take a bus as far as in the desert they would go and then she would ride a camel to the exact coordinates. The bus ride was nearly two and half hours and Miranda was very anxious. She finally got off and then she hopped on a camel and the camel trainer walked along. That ride was almost twice as long as the bus ride but they finally arrived where the treasure was supposedly hidden. As she was riding along on the camel, she heard a really hard hollow thump. She immediately jumped off and looked around on the ground. She had actually found an underground tunnel that lead to the treasure. She was so excited she screamed and jumped up and down with joy. Miranda had found the treasure that she had longed for almost her entire life.

Miranda moved on along with the treasure and went to look for her father; she hoped that he was still okay and luckily not far away. As she came closer to the coordinates, she saw someone. It was her father, and she ran up to him. The gravediggers had already left him because he would not give them any hints on where was the treasure. Miranda and Jonathan left the desert with the treasure and once they arrived home, took it to the museum. They became famous, and received a large reward. Miranda went back to school and became a professor on Egyptian history. She got married and lived happily ever after.

# CHAPTER 13

## THE MYSTERY OF KAMCHATKA

In a small village on Kamchatka (nuclear testing zone in Russia), there has been a mysterious disappearance in the village for the past 13 weeks. There have been bloody paw prints around the crime scenes that are unknown. They had no idea what it could be. There were 13 toes on the animal's feet. They have found big samples of its fur and the creature seemed to be an origin of the brown bear. There have been a total of 12 disappearances. We have found 5 corpses and 2 people in a coma, the rest of the bodies were not found. We are MIG (Mutation International Group) and we will not stop until we find the beast. We have formed a search group and are tracking this creature. We have a total of 19 samples of fur, skin and markings in which we found samples of radioactivity which were also found in each of the victim's blood. The radioactivity must be caused by the nuclear testing in the area.

This morning we put together another squad of professional animal trackers and radioactivity experts to search and capture this beast. The squad reported sightings around 8 pm till 2 am. The beast is about 9 feet tall. We have set infra red cameras and bait close to the last 5 sightings. We have seen numerous animals pass by but none of them were our subject. Later that night one squad was attacked by the beast with one casualty but luckily one of the squad members shot the beast with a tranquilizer gun. The creature got away and dart seemed to do nothing to the beast. The next morning we deployed another squad to retrieve the beast. We found it lying in a den. We took the beast to a testing room in the MIG headquarters. After we did some testing we found out it was just a bear that had been exposed to radioactivity. Eight hours later the bear escaped. Nobody knows how he got through security but he is out on the loose and is yet to be recaptured. If there are any suspicious sightings please contact MIG at 1-800-BEAR-NOW.

# CHAPTER 14

## WHO ROBBED THE BANK

It was 12:01 am at the Bank of America and this night was not like every night. There was a boom at the entrance of the bank. Cops were there guarding. It was dark, and they began falling one after one hitting the floor. They were not dead just knocked out cold.

Next at 5:00 A.M. News 13 went to the Bank of America interviewing the manager and the people at the front desk. News 13 was questioning how many people had robbed the bank and how much money had been stolen. The manager and the people at the front desk replied "two people had robbed the bank and they had stolen $20,000 dollars." Chanel 13 was surprised that two people could pull a stunt like this considering that the bank was very well guarded by police officers. So later on at about 6:00 A.M. the manager decided to call a detective but since he wasn't available the CSI team came.

At 7:00 am the CSI team arrived at the scene of the robbery. They were investigating what had happened with the cops and wondered who had done it. They had four prime suspects and one witness. But the witness was not talking.

At 7:45 am the witness started talking after the CSI team convinced him. He said that at 6:00 a.m. he was withdrawing some money from the bank when he heard a boom. Then that's when he blacked out after that he doesn't know. Until he heard someone say to take the $20,000 dollars to Elm Street. He also said that the second man that robbed the bank was tall, thin, short hair, tan and wore a red jacket. That was all the CSI team needed to know to find this man and put him in jail.

The CSI had half of the case solved. One of the men who robbed the bank had been put in jail, and part of the money had been returned to the bank. Now there was only one last mad man left on the streets and $13,000 dollars left.

The question is who robbed the bank and how did he rob it. There are four suspects, that have robbed the bank that night and they were Dallas, Manuel, Shawn and Tristan.

Dallas was watching America' Funniest Home Videos at 12:01 a.m., Manuel was frying some chicken for dinner at 12:01 a.m., Shawn was looking at a goldfish at 12:01 a.m. and Tristan was sleeping at the same time. Or so that's what they said, but we knew that Dallas, Manuel and Shawn were not lying. So only one person was the guilty one and that was Tristan.

Tristan was taken to court, and arrested for the robbery and knocking out cops. He received 17 years in jai.

# CHAPTER 15

## WHO KILLED THE MUFFIN MAN

Once upon a time, there was a very fat baker who lived on Blueberry lane. He had a dream about a new recipe for muffins that he could sell at his shop. The muffin was more like a cupcake. It was a chocolate muffin with a chocolate filling inside with chocolate chips on top. It was going to be called the triple chocolate layer muffin. So after the inspiring dream he decided to go down to his store to try out the new recipe. A gingerbread man walked in. The gingerbread man was 5 feet tall and still decided to order a dozen of the new muffins. The muffin man was very excited and all the 305 pounds of him jumped up and down eagerly and not paying attention he added 2 cups of salt in the batter instead of chocolate extract. Then the muffin man put them in the oven and set the timer for 5 minutes, but all the salt drained the puffy muffins moisture making them burn faster and taste even more disgusting. When the timer rang, the muffin man was so excited that he did not even look at the muffins when they came out, and he just threw the plate of muffins on the table and went back to the kitchen. The little gingerbread man took a bite and was so furious for having spent 4 dollars on muffins that tasted repulsive, and it had broken all his gumball teeth. When the muffin man came out to see how he was doing, the gingerbread man threw the muffins at the muffin man and kicked him unconscious and tons of rock hard muffins went in his mouth and chocked him to death. When he fell down he made so a loud vibration that people all the way to China could hear. Lots of people came into the shop and found him down on the ground.

After the devastating crime, police were searching everywhere until they found 30 broken gumball teeth on the floor. They figured the only guy who had those teeth was the gingerbread man so the police went to his cottage up in the fruit lane. They knocked at the door and his wife answered. They asked for the gingerbread man to come out, they had to speak to him. She said she had not seen him since he went to the muffin shop. The cops found a frosting trail loading to the woods and from there they searched for days until the trail came to an end. Police put out flyers of the man, with blue frosting eyes, and gum drop buttons. A week later a little girl spotted the gingerbread cookies next to the man. They ran up arrested him with tiny handcuffs and took him to jail.

He was sentenced to 10 years in prison, and I guess that is what happens when you throw a giant plate of muffins at a fat man.

# CHAPTER 16

## ALIEN VISITORS

"What should we do with him?" said a mysterious voice.

"We should leave him there, his memory is wiped out."

The two odd looking strange creatures left the room and the door shut behind them

Two hour later I woke up and opened my eyes, a blinding light hit me and I could barely see. I looked down at my stomach and saw a huge scar stitched together. The scar stretched from the top of my chest all the way down to my belly-bottom. I also had a severe migraine. A pain surged through my body and it went from head to toes and it was unbearable. By the looks of my surrounding I could tell that I was being held captive. I could also tell that escape did not seem like an option since there was a blue energy field all around me. I touched it and my hand hurt really badly but strangely enough it was not an electric shock, but something else.

Then all of a sudden a flashing red light went off, an alarm assaulted my eardrums making me half deaf. I saw about 10 guards rushing towards what looked like a control room. The energy field fell and I got out. I heard gunshots and explosions that did not sound like weapon from earth. A voice from behind me said, "Sergeant Conner,"

"Yes, that is me but, who are you?"

"I am your ticket out of this place, call me Anne. Here use this rifle."

She tossed me the gun and we stepped out of the room and turned left. Immediately we saw the nine alien creatures that looked like warriors, with heavy looking armor. We took aim and where about to fire but someone else beat us to the punch and nine golden buckets whizzed by and slammed against the door but missing the aliens. They quickly turned and fired back at the assailants.

Conner yelled, "Could someone tell me what's going on!"

"You mean, you don't know,?" said Anne. "We are in war with the alien species, the dryads. They are visitors to our world and we must stop them. Those three soldiers are the leaders of the alien race and our way off this ship."

"Why are these aliens so special?" Asked Conner.

"Well first of all, they can only be killed with gold bullets. Second, each of those leaders has a key to unlock a door that leads to the alien mother who gives birth to all the soldiers and makes weapon for them," said Anne.

"Our soldiers aren't afraid to die; the only thing they are afraid of is losing this war. Let's get back to headquarters."

"No", argues Connor.

Anne asked, "Why not?"

"I am starting to remember things now; they killed my wife and my son. This has been going on for 5 years. I must stop it now."

I ran down the hallway and looked at the three soldiers. I fired three times and killed all of them and took the keys. I went to the big room in the center of the ship; I opened the door and saw the basement which had three key holes. I put the keys slowly in the door . . . AHHHHH . . . "What a terrible dream," yelled Connor.

# CHAPTER 17

## THE SULLIVAN ROBBERY

On a crisp autumn morning, as the birds were chirping, Robert M. Sullivan headed to work at the S&J Law firm in Beverly Hills. For the past few weeks, Robert has been accusing Dalton Robinson for robbing the jewelry store down the road. As Robert strictly strolled in, he pondered about his beautiful wife Nancy, which he met due to his partnership with her father. To his surprise, he gets an urgent phone call from his wife reporting that her father had tragically died. Robert was also informed that Nancy's step mother Nina will inherit all the money. This fact made Nancy cringe with anger.

This had shocked Robert; he thought his partner had been in perfect condition for his age. He was deeply saddened and was worried about operating the business by himself. On the other hand, Robert tried to look at the positive side, that Nancy's father would have been proud to let Robert run the business and become wealthier. Nancy of course, knew this information as well. Robert went through the day contemplative and right as he got into the car, he got a phone call from his security company. His house had been broken into. Robert felt frightened for his family, but then quickly remembered his kids were at a friend's house and Nancy had gone shopping. He asked the security company what had been taken from it. The answer sent a shiver up Robert's spine. Approximately five-hundred million dollars in jewels, paints, vases and money had been stolen. Robert felt weak in the knees and hung up the phone. He told his driver to take him to the beach where he preferred to sit and think awhile.

Right when Robert arrived he got a phone call from the police department. The detectives told him that they thought Dalton had robbed his house. Robert thanked them and said goodbye.

In Detective Mark's office, a letter sat on his desk. The detective opened the letter and saw it contained two clues, number 14 and number 1, signalizing the robbery of Robert M. Sullivan's home.

Detective Mark dismissed it because he was sure it was Dalton. A few days went by and no leads emerged from questioning Dalton Robinson when another letter arrived. This one had two other clues the number 14 and 3. Again, the detective dismissed the letter. A few more days went by and still no leads. A week went by and Detective Mark wondered why he couldn't connect Dalton to the case. He decided to work on the clues. The next clue showed up the next day. The clue was two. It was 25 . . . . Detective Mark though of ways the numbers 14, 1, 14, 3, and 25 could work into a clue. Then he got a wonderful idea . . . the alphabet.

Nancy! The letters spelled out Nancy, Robert's wife! All Detective Mark had to do was incorporate the alphabet. The court became puzzled at this new piece of information. The police checked and rechecked the series of clues. Every time the problems were reworked the detectives and policemen found the same answer. Nancy Elle Sullivan, Robert M. Sullivan's wife robbed her own house? None of this made sense. The court decided to bring in several neighbor to see if they knew anything.

Finally, one of the neighbors told his tale, "I saw Nancy walking out of the house with a bag on the night of the robbery. It had to be her. The robbery was reported shortly after she fled the scene. I didn't want anyone to know."

The neighbor told the court. The court told the neighbor that his name would remain anonymous. The court felt they must bring Nancy to the stand to question her. Nancy acted oddly and finally the information tumbled out of her. It turned out that Nancy despised Robert, her own husband. Nancy had married Robert for his money and when Nancy found out that she wouldn't inherit any money from her father's death, she had taken action. When Robert became the full owner of the firm and instantly received more money, Nancy decided to rob him. Dalton's record was cleared of the charges from the robbery in Robert's house. Nancy was sentenced to two years in prison. Robert was shocked that his wife hated him, but in the end he found happiness and peace.

# CHAPTER 18

## BACK ALLEY

I walked into my dressing room and sat down by my mirror. I took the feather out of my hair, took off my dress and changed into my normal clothes. I started to do math problems to calm my nerves. Whenever I'm nervous, upset, or excited, I like to do math problems. I've always loved doing math problems ever since I was a little girl.

"Okay, um 18." I said to myself" Oh Easy! Now to the next one"

I heard a voice that gave me the chills. It must be Alex. "Hi, hum you caught me at a bad time." I said like an idiot.

"Just thought I say good night and it's been a pleasure working with you."

He said that like he was in a hurry. He was just sticking his head through the doorway with his hand on the doorknob.

"You are Alex. Umm are you going somewhere because you seem like you are in a hurry to get out of here?"

"Oh, I have to get home that's all. I am just a little tired." Alex said very fast and anxious.

"Okay, then. I'll see you some other time." I said very curiously.

I grabbed my coat and walked out of my dressing room into the long hallway that leads to the back door to the back alley. I walked into the back alley realizing it was really dark. There was a full moon out and no stars. I started walking down the alley to the shortcut I take to my house. Then out of nowhere, Willow, the hobo who lives behind the dumpster in the alley appeared right in front of me. He has been following me for the past six weeks.

"Hi, there Ms. Angelica. I could hear you singing in the play. You were really good," said Willow stroking his long beard.

"Why, thank you," I said kind of scared and creeped out.

"Ms. Angelica, do you know that Alejandro Lopez man?" Willow stated.

"Yes, why? did you see him pass by Willow?" I said very scared.

"He walked around the left corner to the alley next door and he was meeting this young woman."

"Thank you, Willow." I shouted as I was running down the alley to the left corner. I stopped by the corner of the alley to take a peak down the next alley to the left. I looked down the alley and to my surprise I saw Alex and Carol-Anne hugging and kissing. I felt my stomach starting to turn as I saw the man I was crazy for kissing another woman. I felt a tear come down my cheek.

I thought of a problem in my head as I watched the two love birds. Even a math problem did not cheer me up this time.

I saw Alex's hands around Carole-Anne neck and he was smiling.

"I really like you Carol-Anne;" said Alex smiling.

"I really like you too," said Carol-Anne.

"I have to go, Alex."

"Can I come with you?" said Alex

"Sorry my mom is staying with me and I have to get home. I will meet you back here tomorrow at 08:00 p.m."

Alex said, "Okay, I can't wait."

He kissed her once more and left.

I went over to her, "Hi there", I said to Carol-Anne.

"Oh, hi. I loved your show tonight. My name is Carol-Anne," she said sticking out her hand smiling.

I grabbed here, "I'm Angelica Green. Do you want to see something really cool?"

"Yes", she said.

"Follow me then."

I looked at her face and noticed she was blushing. I was so mad at her. I wanted to do something so badly I couldn't control it. "I am going to do it, everyone is going to have to deal with it." I thought.

I woke up with a loud knock at my door. I opened it and noticed it was Alex in tears.

"What's wrong?" I asked.

"She is dead. Carol-Anne is dead. They found her body in Grand Central Park along with this book of math problems."

He held out a purple book that had a picture of Shirley Temple doing math problems. I then realized it was mine. I had left it there after I had killed Carol-Anne.

"Why are you so upset? Did you like her?"

"I did know her, Angelica. Last night we kissed in the back alley. I really liked her."

I was so mad at Carol Anne still even after I killed her.

"Im sorry Alex. I did not know."

"It is okay. No one knew."

I felt so guilty but also proud.

"I am going down to Grand Central park. Do you want to come with me?" Alex was crying.

"No, I am kind of tired so I am going back to bed. I might later though." I said looking at my hands.

"Okay, good bye and I am sorry I woke you up."

I just nodded and waved at him. Alex left with a puddle of tears in his eyes. I went back to bed and had a dream about last night. I had lead Carol-Anne into the park and pushed her into a tree. Then I started to do math problems and I did not answer the last one on the last page. No one else can do those problems but me. I am dead. I woke up screaming around my big room and feel asleep instantly.

"Hello Chief. Do you know how she died?" Alex said.

"Yes, the killer pushed her into a tree and she died of head injury." The chief of police said.

"Who did this?" Alex asked.

"A woman who is very good at math. She answered all the questions on the book that she left behind. Do you know anyone?"

"I know exactly who did it. Chief please, come with me."

Once again Angelica was awaken by a loud knock. She answered and again it was Alex looking very curious.

"Angelica can you answer this question please?"

"Uhm, it is very simple, here the answer is 12. Why did you want to know the answer?"

I was getting scared and nervous.

"I wanted proof that you killed Carol-Anne and you just gave it to me. Why did you kill her.?'

"I was jealous that you liked her more than me,"

"Sheriff, come in, arrest her."

There was the sheriff and I was dragged to the car. Alex sat in front very furious and upset.

Next I had to write a confession.

Alex left.

It was the last time I saw him

# CHAPTER 19

## WHY THE WATER CRIES

One day the sultan and his visir went for a walk in the woods. When they arrived to the place they picked up some wood and made a nice fire, they also took water from the river and boiled it.

While the water was boiling, they heard someone sing and cry.

"What is the water saying?" Asked the sultan.

But he did not know what to answer.

The sultan got angry and said," If you cannot tell me what the water is saying, I will have your head. Go, you have forty days to find out."

The visir scared and worried, tried to find someone that would tell him what the water was saying. But where? He put some old clothes on and went around to different places. People would give him food, but when he asked the question, they would look at him like he was crazy.

One day he asked a woodsman, but he could not tell him the answer. The visir had a message for him.

He said, "Thank your daughter, tell her that the year has eleven months, the moon is not full and the ocean is not full."

The woodsman went home and told the daughter the message, she got angry, "But father, what have you done?'"

The woodsman confessed, "I was hungry, and I ate an egg, bread and drank some water."

The visir thought, "Certainly this girl would be able to tell me what the water was saying."

When he saw the woodsman and his daughter, the visir said, "Please, girl, tell what the water is saying and what the fire is singing, otherwise the sultan will have my head cut off."

"I will not tell you, but I will tell the sultan in person."

So they left to go to the sultan. The sultan said, "Tell me girl, what is the water saying when is on the fire."

She answered, "My king, I will tell you only after you marry me."

The sultan did not want to really marry her, but the wise men told him to do it, so to save the visir's life.

After the wedding, he asked his wife, "Now, please tell, what the water was saying."

And the girl, "The water was saying, 'I was here first, I run in the river, I give water to the trees and their roots, and then the fire burns the trees. The water is trying to tell you, that she has been so generous to the woods that you were burning, and this is her reward."

The sultan was pleased with the answer and said, "Now you are really my wife."

# CHAPTER 20

## MARY AND JOHN

One day Mary, the last of two sisters and twelve brothers, went to the lake. She got wet and went ashore. But as she was trying to put her clothes back on she found a snake in her shirt.

She was scared, tried to throw the snake away, but the snake started talking and told her that he will go away only if the young woman would promise to marry him.

Mary did not know what to say, she was so scared that she finally accepted so that she could dress and go home.

Days went by, nothing was happening, till the young girl's house was invaded by snakes, they wanted to ask her parents the permission to the wedding.

Mary's parents were terrified and they agreed, so Mary was taken away to the lake and there was a handsome young man that told her that he was the snake in her shirt.

They left and went to an island, where there was a castle and their future home. They married and had three boys and a girl.

Nine years passed and Mary had forgotten her parents. One day, the oldest son asked about his grandparents, "Mother, I would like to meet them." She asked her spouse, John if she could go with her children to visit her parents.

John agreed but first she had to tess an entire distaff of silk. Mary, started working and days went by but was taking too long. So she asked help to a good witch. The good witch told her to throw the distaff in the fire after she had finished. Mary obeyed and went to John. "My dear husband, I have finished what you requested. May I please leave?"

"My dear wife," said John, "I have decided to give you a pair of shoes, and you will go only when the bottom is completed gone."

When Mary put the shoes on, she realized that the bottom was made of iron. She walked, walked but the iron was still there. So she went to a shoe man and he helped her.

Happily she went to her husband, and he said, "My dear wife, now you can leave. Bring some present for your parents. First prepare a beautiful cake"

But John had hided all the pots and pans. Mary was desperate, again she asked help to the fairy, and was able to finish the cake.

John could not think of anything else, so he took his wife and children to the lake and told Mary what to sing so he could come and get her. He also told his children not to say a word.

Mary and the children left; saw her parents and friends, they were so happy that they did not realize that nine days had gone by.

Mary's family did not want for her to leave and tried to find out information on the song that Mary was supposed to sing to get John back. They took the two boys in the woods, but they refused to tell the words. The smallest girl was so scared that told the whole thing.

Mary's brothers went to the lake, called John and as soon as they saw him, they killed him.

Mary had no idea of what had happened. She said goodbye to her parents and with her children went to the lake and started singing.

"John, John, if you are alive, foam of milk.

If you are dead, foam of blood."

As soon as she had finished singing, blood appeared, and then she heard John's voice. What had happened?

Mary, with a broken heart cried. John said "Your daughter will became a poplar, your leaves will trembles night and day, the rain will wash your little face and the wind will comb your hair. You, my sons will be strong trees, and your mother a Pine tree".

And so happened

# CHAPTER 21

## THE LANDOWNER, THE SHEPERD AND THE KING

Once upon a time lived a very rich landowner, one day he wrote on a tablet, "If someone knows what misery yes, please have him explain it to me." Then he took the tablets and nailed it on a tree on the board of the road.

A king came by, saw the tablet and he thought, 'I will show him what misery means'.

The next day he called the landowner and asked him, "Do you know how much the moon weighs? How much a king is worth? Where is the center of the world? How many stars are in the sky and how many stories have you told."

The landowner did not now what to say. The king gave him three days to think about.

The landowner went home; he was very worried and started walking around.

A shepherd, who was with calves and pigs in the field, saw his owner so worried and asked him what was the problem.

The landowner said, "I am worried, I don't know how to answer the king's questions."

The Shepherd then proposed that he would go to the king and answer the questions. The landowner accepted his offer.

The king, saw the shepherd, and asked the same questions. The shepherd answered. "The moon weighs one pound because like the pound is divided in 4 parts. The king is worth 15 coins, because if Christ, king of the sky and earth, was sold for 30 coins, it was fair for the king to be worth half of it. The center of the world was where they were standing, and the stars in the sky were five hundred."

The king told him "You are lying, no way you knew the answers."

The shepherd said, "If the king does not believe me, he can count them."

The king realized that the boy had won so he asked for one last thing. "Tell me a story that I have not heard before."

The boy said, "There was a man that was taking his pigs out and was talking with his king."

The king liked the boy, send away the landowner from his land and send him to take care of the pigs.

The shepherd received the land and still lives there.

Now the landowner knew what misery was.

# CHAPTER 22

## WAR

By: Alessandra Kutz

The war is not jovial and bright,
The troops going there may experience a sight.
We have political debates about the War in Iraq,
Half of them say the troops should come back,
The troops are shipped off to many locations,
If it's Kabul or Baghdad they're still not on vacation.
You may sign-up at age seventeen,
They want us to have freedom, it certainly seems.
They're doing great what can I say,
Defending my country and giving us the freedom to live day by day.
Seeing the sights that they see must be scary,
Those sights they see must differ and vary.
What they go through, I just can't believe,
What they do there they really do achieve.
Parents say goodbye to their daughter or son,
Knowing they give me freedom, I thank each and every one.
They're doing fantastic at what they best do,
All I can say really is Thank You.

# CHAPTER 23

## MOTHER'S DAY

By: David Womack Wills

Like all the fathers want to say,
To you a Happy Mother's Day
As everyone know I've ever found
Rose is the bestest Mother Mopa around.
This card's to you from Heaven above
Covered with kisses and full of love!
I'm fortunate to have found you
And lucky to have bound you.
My love, my girl and best friend, too
I cannot show all my love for you
(The first of cards for the next 20 years)

# CHAPTER 24

## MOTHER'S DAY

By: David Womack Wills

I really don't mean to bug you
I surely would rather just hug you
Mother's Day is here again
My love and congratulations I send
Take the gifts, use them I say
To create at school a big display
I hope we make another thirty-seven
Unless I leave and go to heaven
Best still I stay and wait for you
Because our love is so very true

Gobs of Love
Dave

# CHAPTER 25

## MAN'S CREATION

It was a dark but starry night; a group of Indians were sitting around a fire. Suddenly the oldest warrior stood up. His face was old and dark like the earth and he was wearing a very colorful blanket. He started narrating the history of the world.

When the Coyote, the dog of the desert, finished creating the world, he took the wind, which was in the shape of a shell, and turned it inside out and formed the sky. He send the different colors to the five parts of the world and a rainbow went into the sky and divided into day and night.

Coyote also refilled the planes with trees, rivers, mountains, ponds and created also all the animals.

Then he said, "Now I'm going to create Man."

The animals heard and wanted to help. So they all sit in a circle in the forest; Coyote, Grizzly **Bear,** the Lion, the Blonde bear, the Deer, the Sheep, the beaver, the owl and the Mouse.

The Lion said, "You can create the Man in any form that you like, but I think he should have teeth so he can eat meat, and also long paws."

"Like yours?" asked Coyote.

"Well, yes, like mine," answered the Lion.

"He is also going to need fur and a very strong voice."

"Like yours," asked the Coyote again.

"Yes, like mine," answered the Lion.

"No one wants a voice like yours," the Grizzly Bear interrupted.

"Every one runs away, when they hear you. Man needs to walk with paws on the back, so he can pick objects in front of him and crush them."

"Like you?" asked Coyote.

"Yes, like the way I do." Answered the Grizzly Bear.

The Deer was shacking very nervously, and looking over his shoulder. He said, "Why are you talking about eat meat and destroy things? This is not nice. Man needs to know when he is in danger so he can run away. He should have ears like the sea shells so he can ear every little noise; and eyes like the moon, so he can see every where; and of course horns, he definitely needs horns."

"Like yours?" asked Coyote.

"Well, yes, like mine", answered the Deer.

"Like yours?" laughed the Sheep.

"While would he need horns? Horns get caught in branches and plants. Instead he should have two small horns at the side of his head?"

"Like yours?" asked Coyote.

The Sheep, was very offended, she did not like to be interrupted.

Then the Beaver said, "You forgot the most important thing, the tail. Tails long and thin can send away flies. But a man needs a large and flat tail. How is he going to build dams in the river?"

"Like yours?" asked Coyote.

"No one can build dam as good as I do," answered the Beaver.

"Listen to me," said the Mouse.

"The Man you want is too big, make a smaller one."

"You are all crazy," screamed the Owl.

"And wings? Have you not thought about wings? If you want the Man to be better than animals, he must be able to fly. He must have wings."

"Like you?" asked Coyote.

"Is this all you can say?" said the Owl.

"Don't you have ideas of your own?"

Coyote jumped on his feet and advanced towards the circle of animals.

"You are all stupid animals. I have no idea why I created all of you. You want Man to be like you."

"Oh, so you want him to look like you?" said the Bear.

"How would we be able to distinguish each other." Said the Coyote.

"Every one can point at me, and say, 'here is Man', and then point to Man and say' here is Coyote. No, No, No. Man must be different."

"But the wings!" said the Owl.

"But the horns!" said the Deer.

"But the small horns" said the Sheep.

"But the strong voice!" said the Grizzly Bear.

"But being small!" said the mouse.

"And without tail,!" said the Beaver.

They all started fighting, biting each other, the animals were fighting, while Coyote was looking and shacking his head. Feathers and fur, nails, pieces of horns were every where. Coyote picked them up, put them all together and created the Camel and the Giraffe.

Soon all animals, tired to fight fell down.

"I think I have the answer," said Coyote.

The animals looked at him, some snarled, but Coyote kept on talking.

"Bear is right, Man should walk on two legs, so he can climb trees. The deer is right that he should have a very sharp sight and hearing. But he cannot have wings because he will crash in the sky. But he does need long extremities like the eagle. We will call these fingers. The lion is right he should have a strong voice. But he also needs a soft voice so he will not scare everyone. Man should be smooth like a fish, so he would not be too hot with fur. The most important thing, he needs to be more intelligent and shrewd than all of you.

"Like you," said all the animals.

"Yes, thank you," answered Coyote.

"Like me."

They all screamed and finally said, "Sit down, Coyote. We do not like your ideas".

"Okay," said Coyote.

"Let's compete. All of you by tomorrow make an example of Man out of mud. We will look and decide which one is the best."

The animals all ran to the river got some sand and water. The Owl made one with wings, the deer one with long horns and big eyes. Beaver made one with a large and flat tail and the mouse a small one.

But Coyote made Man. He was the first one to finish. So they all went to the forest to sleep. All except Coyote. He took water from the river, and put some on the tail, and it disappeared, some on the horns and they disappeared and some on the wings. Then he blew in the nose of his model, and when they all woke up they found a new animal in the forest. His name was Man.

The old warrior sat down, and put his blanket around him. The fire was about to extinguish, it was dark, and far away you could hear the scream of the coyote.

# CHAPTER 26

## NINETY-NINE CHICKENS AND ONE ROOSTER

Once upon a time there was a family that lived in a farm. There was a husband, wife and many animals, mostly chickens, ninety nine chickens and only one rooster.

One day the husband said to his wife," We have so many chickens why we do not sell some of them?"

The wife agreed and the next day she went to the market to sell to a man who was looking for a good business.

But the man said, "I do not have the money to pay you, I will leave you a rooster as promise, but please let me use your donkey to transport the chickens."

The woman agreed.

The man:" How about the dog, in case someone tries to steal my chickens?"

The woman gave him anything he asked, and in the evening when she went back home told her husband the whole story. The husband started screaming, he was so angry. The next day he left looking for women that he could deceive.

On the road he saw a girl next to a well. He approached her. The young woman asked, "Where are you coming from?"

He answered, "I am coming from the world of the dead."

The girl said, "Do you know John?. He was the poor dear son of my boss."

"Of course, I know him, he is fine but poor. He needs shoes, money and clothes."

The girl ran to her boss. When the man heard he gave the man food, money anything for his dead son.

In the evening the woman's husband came home. He was an officer of the king. The woman told him about the son and that she had given to the man everything that the dead son wanted.

The officer knew it was a scam and went to look for the man. The man saw it coming and he hided next to a windmills and told the miller. "Run, someone is looking for you." The poor miller ran on top of a tree and covered himself with flour. Soon the officer came and asked the miller (who was the thief), to keep his horse while he looked for him. The officer jumped off the horse, climbed the tree, the thief took his boots, his horse and ran away with the money.

The officer went back home, sorry for not having found the thief, but he did not want to tell his wife, so he said, "You gave away for our dead son shoes, clothes and money, and I gave him also my boots and the horse."

# CHAPTER 27

## THE SNAIL

Once upon a time there was a snail that for boredom walked around. One day she came out of a bunch of garbage and she found a copper coin. It was dirty, but the snail cleaned it and the coin was shining again.

"What could I buy," she thought. Finally she decided to buy things that were necessary for survival.

"But this is boring; I am going to buy something that will make me pretty". So she purchased some lipstick and eye shadow. She started walking around, and a farmer saw her. "Where are you going ugly snail?"

"Why are you calling me ugly? I am beautiful. Call me beautiful and dressy."

The farmer agreed, and then asked her where she was going.

"To sell myself."

"Well, then come with me, I am buying you."

But before she would accept, she asked him how he beat his wife.

"With a pitchfork, of course, that is what I always have in my hands."

"Sorry, I am not interested" and the snail kept on walking.

Many others approached her, and she would ask the same questions. Finally she met a mouse. A beautiful mouse with beautiful fur. He asked the snail where she was going.

The rat was smart, so when she asked him how he beat his wife, he answered, "I do not beat her, I caress her with my tail."

The snail fell in love and decided to marry the mouse.

Many months later she was busy cleaning the house and she fell in a hole. She was terrorized, she screamed and asked a passerby, "Please help me. I am at the bottom of the hole. Please go get my husband, he is a mouse with a pretty tail. Tell him his beautiful wife is in danger."

The mouse came right away, but was annoyed and told his wife, "Come on, do not let me waste time, give me your hand and I will get you up, I am in a hurry."

The snail was mortified and said, "You ugly mouse, you are already tired of me."

The husband was already angry, so he left her in the hole and walked away, and you can still see her at the bottom the hole.

# CHAPTER 28

## MOVE AWAY FROM MY HEART

Move away from my heart, it is not going to be very difficult
Let me see if life is possible without the feelings of your arms, your skin,
your face

Move away from my heart, we are not the first one nor we are going to
be the last ones.
You must abandon me, I can't defend myself from memories, your touch
and all the usual
things that before were uniting us and now they are dividing us.

Move away from my heart and take away my nightmares
It takes so little to destroy all the work that has taken us to love, when
there is no dream
To reach and no star to follow.

What a discretions, almost unspeakable, while in these rooms there is
only unbearable
Silence that's too heave to carry, what we have lost is the fear to lose.

Go away from my heart, let's try living again.

# CHAPTER 29
## THE POOR AND ONE THOUSAND PIECES

This man was poor, very poor, and he worked the whole day. Like him, his wife and children were dead tired every night. But in spite of this, after dinner, the neighbor that was thinking he should be tired that they would fall asleep, he could head noises of celebrations.

"Take the guitar papa," the smallest of his children would say.

"Play the song from yesterday," would say the other son smiling.

The wife would place all the chairs in a circle, take one of her daughters in her arms, give her a toy, and then make her go up and down on her knees. The father would start playing, and for two hours they would forget their poverty and how tired they were.

"Do you remember this song?" the father would ask.

"Go ahead, sing the first verse Peter . . ."

Next to them lived a very rich man, and he was bothered by the music and the laughing of this family. He would think, "I have every thing that a man could desire, good food, ten cooks. I have everything. Ten cars, boats. Everything. But they are, dancing, they have nothing and they are happy. I am going to give them some money, let's see if they can be any happier."

The next day the rich man knocked at the door of the poor man.

"My dear neighbor. You are an honest man. You deserve some money. Take this and be happy, use them as you wish."

"Thank you, but you do not have to . . . ."

"No, don't say anything. Your family makes me happy. I hear you every night. Is my gratitude to you."

The poor man, went inside and was thinking what to do with the money. He had many ideas, but none seemed very good. So much money in my house.

"Should we buy a vineyard?' he asked his wife.

"But dear, I am fine, they way I am, I love you . . ."

"I love you to, but we need to do something with this money."

The youngest son said, "Where is the guitar, papa?."

"The guit . . . oh please, look I am busy right now. Go to your room, no guitar tonight. Am I the only one worried of what to do with this money."

That was the first night that no one danced or sung. The children were very sad, the wife on the verge of tears. The man was quiet for four days, only thinking about the money.

Then he looked at his children, and decided. Without hesitation he went to the next door neighbor and gave him the money back and said, "I thank you, my dear neighbor, now I know what happiness is, and it has nothing to do with money."

That night the music started again, and never stopped.